Preventive Health Care
for Pet Birds

Preventive Health Care for Pet Birds
The Essentials for a Healthy Bird

Dr. Greg Burkett, Dipl. ABVP (Avian)

Copyright © 2020 Greg Burkett

All rights reserved.

No part of this publication in print or in electronic format may be reproduced, stored in a retrieval system, or transmitted in any form or by any means, electronic, mechanical, photocopying, recording, or otherwise without the prior written permission of the publisher.

Distributed by Bublish, Inc.

ISBN: 978-1-64704-111-3

Table of Contents

INTRODUCTION 3

BIRD CARE ESSENTIALS 5
   FORMULATED PELLET DIET: THE IMPORTANCE OF A
   PROPER DIET.. 6
   Why to Convert Your Bird to a Formulated Pellet Diet. 7
   How to Convert Your Bird to a Formulated Pellet Diet 8
      Steps of the Conversion Method 8
      Some Helpful Hints to Coax Conversion to Pellets 9
      Some Important Points to Remember When Converting to
      Pellets.. 10
   For Diet, Do Not 10
   CAGE: THE IMPORTANCE OF A CAGE 11
   Choosing the Right Cage.. 15
      Qualities of a good cage 15
      Guidelines for Minimum Cage Size and Maximum Bar Spacing. 15
   For Cages, Do not 16
   Furnishing the Cage with Bird Care Essentials......................... 18
      Perches 18
      Food Dishes.. 19
      Water bottle 19
      Toys 19
      Foraging Feeders and Foraging Toys 19
      Substrate 20
   For Furnishing the Cage, Do Not 20
   Setting up Your Bird's Cage.. 20
   Cage Location 23
   For Cage Location, Do Not... 23
   Cleaning and Disinfecting the Cage... 24

For Cleaning and Disinfecting Your Cage, Do Not........................25
PERCHES: THE IMPORTANCE OF PERCHES 25
   For Perches, Do Not 26
WATER BOTTLE: THE IMPORTANCE OF WATER BOTTLES 27
   Why to Convert Your Bird to a Water Bottle.............................27
   How to Convert Your Bird to a Water Bottle............................29
   For Water Sources, Do Not 30
TRAY LINER: THE IMPORTANCE OF FLAT PAPER TRAY LINERS 30
   For Tray Liners, Do not 30
TOYS: THE IMPORTANCE OF TOYS 31
FORAGING FEEDERS: THE IMPORTANCE OF FORAGING................... 32
LIGHTING: THE IMPORTANCE OF FULL-SPECTRUM LIGHTING......... 33
   For Lighting, Do not..34
PLAY GYM: THE IMPORTANCE OF A PLAY GYM 35
CARRIER: THE IMPORTANCE OF A CARRIER..................................... 35
GRAM SCALE: THE IMPORTANCE OF A GRAM SCALE 35

VETERINARY CARE: THE IMPORTANCE OF VETERINARY CARE 37
   WHAT IS AN AVIAN VETERINARIAN AND WHY DOES MY BIRD
      NEED ONE? 38
   ANNUAL WELL- BIRD CHECKUPS 38
   HOW TO KNOW WHEN YOUR BIRD IS SICK,
      AND WHEN TO SEE AN AVIAN VETERINARIAN.......................... 42
      Signs of a Sick Bird...46
      For Veterinary Care, Do Not 47

AVIAN FIRST AID: BE YOUR BIRD'S FIRST RESPONDER 51
   EMERGENCY SITUATIONS REQUIRING IMMEDIATE
      VETERINARY ATTENTION 52
   EMERGENCY SITUATIONS REQUIRING SAME-DAY
      VETERINARY ATTENTION 52
   HOW TO MANAGE EMERGENCY SITUATIONS 53
      The First Aid Kit 53
      Hospital Cage..53
      What To Do In An Emergency...54
      General Supportive Care 55

 Emergencies Requiring First Aid 55
  Animal Attacks 56
  Bleeding 56
  Breathing Difficulties 58
  Burns 59
  Egg Binding 60
  Eye Problems 60
  Fractures 61
  Head Trauma 62
  Heatstroke (Hyperthermia) 62
  Sick Bird Syndrome 63
  Toxin Inhalation 64
  Toxin Ingestion 65
  For First Aid, Do Not 66

ENVIRONMENTAL TOXINS 69
 Heavy Metals 70
  Zinc 70
  Lead 72
 Toxic Foods 73
 Tobacco 74
 Teflon and other Non-stick Surfaces 74
  Common Items Having Toxic Non-stick Coatings 75
 Plants 76
  Toxic Plants 76
  Safe Plants 77
 Mite Protectors and Sprays 79

PROPER HANDLING AND TRAINING 81
 Wing Clipping 82
  For wing feather clipping, Do not 85
 Handling 85
 Trick Training 86
 Potty Training 86
  For Behavior and Handling, Do Not 88

INDEX 89

Preventive Health Care for Pet Birds
The Essentials for a Healthy Bird

Introduction

The purpose for this book is to describe how to keep a pet bird healthy through preventive health care. There are two categories that support a preventive health care program. The first category is husbandry. Husbandry includes what you feed your bird, how you house your bird, and how you manage your bird's environment. A guideline for good husbandry is the Bird Care Essentials. Items on the Bird Care Essentials list are necessary to provide your bird with the best husbandry preventive health care.

The second category is veterinary care. Having your bird be seen by an avian veterinarian at least annually is vital to a successful preventive health care program. Regular visits to your bird's avian veterinarian will allow the doctor to establish a baseline for all of your bird's health parameters including physical exam, blood work, and X-rays, and an opportunity to see your bird when it is healthy thereby being able recognize when your bird is not healthy. It is also an opportunity to discuss husbandry and make any necessary improvements.

Bird Care Essentials

The Bird Care Essentials are items that are necessary for your bird to remain healthy and are vital to a preventive health care program. They are:

a) Proper diet
b) Large cage
c) Appropriate perches
d) Water bottle
e) Paper tray liner
f) Appropriately sized toys
g) Foraging feeders
h) Full-spectrum lighting
i) Play gym / Training perch
j) Transport carrier
k) Gram scale

Formulated Pellet Diet: The Importance of a Proper Diet

Diet is one of the most important Bird Care Essentials in a preventive health care program. A poor diet is the underlying cause of many health problems in pet birds. A healthy diet needs to be complete and balanced in order to prevent nutritional disease. Formulated pellet diets are made to have all of the nutrients that a bird needs to be healthy with the proper amounts and ratios of each nutrient.

There are two broad categories of food for birds: formulated pellets and treats. If it is not a pellet, then it is a treat. Pet birds like and will eat a variety of foods such as seeds, nuts, rice, beans, pasta, fruits, vegetables, and many other foods. (Figure 1) Generally these foods are healthy for birds but they are only treats. A bird's diet will not be complete and balanced by only feeding a variety of treats, even when adding vitamin supplements to the diet.

Figure 1: Bananas and other fruits are a terrific treat.

Feeding a formulated pellet diet, will guarantee that your bird is eating a complete and balanced diet. Supplements should not be given to birds eating a formulated pellet diet because some nutrients are toxic in excessive amounts. A pet bird's diet should be approximately 90% pellets. The remaining 10% can be any treat. This ratio can be achieved by leaving pellets in the cage at all times and meal feeding treats 2-3 times daily. Treats should be fed in small amounts, enough for one trip to the dish, and then the dish should be removed. Fresh and wet foods should not remain in the cage for more than 2-3 hours because of the potential for bacterial growth.

There are a few exceptions to this pellet to treat ratio. For example, eclectus parrots seem to do better with about 70% pellets and 30% treats, and treats should include fresh vegetables and high protein sources such as eggs, chicken bones, and bee pollen. Other exceptions include budgies, finches, and canaries, which need 20% of their diet to be a good quality seed mix.

WHY TO CONVERT YOUR BIRD TO A FORMULATED PELLET DIET.

Formulated pellet diets have been developed through decades of field research in pet bird nutrition to be a complete and balanced diet, and have been demonstrated to prevent and even cure most nutritional diseases. Pellets are formulated specifically for the needs of a pet bird, which eliminates the need of guessing which supplements are better for your bird and how much of these supplements to provide in an attempt to make a diet complete and balanced. A diet cannot be balanced by adding supplements, and when given incorrectly, supplements can lead to disease caused by nutrient toxicities. Powder supplements are difficult to dose and vitamins in the water should also be avoided because water vitamins cause the growth of harmful bacteria in the water. (Figure 2)

Most importantly, the reasons to convert your bird to a formulated pellet diet are that it will improve your bird's health and prevent nutritional diseases. On a formulated pellet diet your bird will be healthier, happier, and feel better, demonstrating this by being more playful and more active. A pellet diet will also improve the appearance of your bird. Improvements in feather quality are noticeable by feathers being shiny, with brighter more rich colors, and lack of black spots and stress bars (Figure 3). Feathers also become stronger on a formulated pellet diet, which prevents broken feath-

Figure 2: Vitamins in the water can cause life-threatening bacterial infections.

ers and broken blood feathers. Healthy feathers signify a healthy bird. Nails and beaks are stronger and do not grow too long on a formulated pellet diet. Converting your bird to a formulated pellet diet will also add years to your bird's life span. In short, putting your bird on pellets will be the best thing you can ever do for you bird.

Figure 3: Stress bars can be caused by a poor diet.

HOW TO CONVERT YOUR BIRD TO A FORMULATED PELLET DIET

Persistence and consistency are the keys to converting your bird to a new diet. **<u>Do Not Mix Pellets with the Current Diet.</u>** This will prolong the conversion time and your bird will scoop out the food in the dish looking for something they like without eating any pellets.

Steps of the Conversion Method

Step 1. You need to have three food dishes in the cage. One dish should be near the highest perch. The other two dishes should be lower in the cage. Put the pellets in the higher dish and in one of the lower dishes. The current diet will be given in small amounts in the remaining lower dish. The pellets need to be available in the cage at all times and the current diet will be meal-fed two times per day on a set schedule.

Step 2. Establish a routine such that the current diet is given in the morning and in the evening. Give only enough of the current diet to be eaten in one trip to the bowl and do not leave it in the cage overnight. In the afternoon a treat is offered instead of the current diet. The treat can be any food except the current diet. If your bird does not eat other foods, a tablespoon of the current diet should be given. Maintain this routine for 3-4 days. Meanwhile, observe your bird to see if they are consuming the pellets.

Step 3. After 3-4 days, establish a new routine such that you discontinue the current diet in the morning, give the treat in the afternoon, and give the current diet in the evening only. Give only enough of the current diet for one trip to the bowl and do not leave the current diet in the cage overnight. Continue to observe your bird and weigh them daily if possible.

Step 4. After another 3-4 days, discontinue giving the current diet in the evening, and give only the afternoon treat, and the pellets at all times. Most birds will be eating pellets by this stage. Maintain this routine until your bird is eating the new diet.

When you determine that your bird is consuming pellets consistently and maintaining weight, then I recommend that you discontinue the current food completely or feed it as a treat in small amounts.

Some Helpful Hints to Coax Conversion to Pellets

A) It helps to role-play with your bird when you are trying to get them to try new foods. You can be excited and pretend to eat the new food. Offer some of it to someone else in front of your bird, and then offer some to your bird with the same enthusiasm.

B) Birds prefer to eat in flocks. Take your bird out during meal times to dine with you. Have a dish of pellets at the table to offer your bird. Sprinkle some on the table and tap your finger near the food like you are pecking.

C) A dish with a mirror behind it can be a great tool. This works because your bird sees another bird in the mirror eating the food and is more willing to try it. Use the dish with a mirror for the pellets in the high spot for canaries, finches, and budgies. Once the conversion is made the mirror can be removed.

Some Important Points to Remember When Converting to Pellets

A) It is very important to monitor your bird's droppings during and after the conversion process. If the droppings turn to dark green or black, it is an indication that your bird is not eating enough. If not, then give your bird the current diet once daily in the evening, and prolong the conversion process.

B) Weighing your bird is a more accurate method for monitoring during the conversion process. Some weight loss is expected initially, but 10% is the maximum amount of weight loss that is acceptable. If your bird loses 10% or loses three days in a row, then go back a step and prolong the conversion process.

C) The droppings will change during the conversion. This should not be alarming. The droppings may become loose, watery, or may change color. These changes are temporary, but, if they persist, discontinue the conversion process and call your avian veterinarian.

D) You will know your bird is eating when you see crumbles or powder in the dish or on the cage floor. At this point your bird has been converted to pellets, and treats can be reintroduced into the diet in small amounts 2-3 times daily. Continue to weigh your bird and monitor droppings until weight stabilizes and droppings are normal.

FOR DIET, DO NOT

Do not give grit to your bird.
Because parrots do not need grit for digestion, and grit is known to cause intestinal blockage in parrots.
There are no necessary alternatives.

Do not feed chocolate or avocado
Because these food items are fatally toxic to birds.
   Instead feed healthy fruits and vegetables.

Do not feed dairy products
Because birds are lactose intolerant and cannot digest lactose
   Instead offer almond milk or other milk substitute

Do not provide vitamins in your bird's water
Because these are not effective at balancing a diet. They accelerate bacterial growth in the water. They change the taste and smell of the water and your bird may not drink.
   Instead feed a formulated pellet diet and provide healthy treats.

Do not give vitamins and other supplements if your bird is eating pellets
Because pellets are a complete and balanced diet and giving supplements will cause nutrient excesses, which may be toxic to your bird.
   Instead feed a pellet diet and provide healthy treats.

Cage: The Importance of a Cage

A companion pet bird needs a cage. You should provide your bird the best possible home, and respect their home as a place of solitude. A common misconception is that a cage is just for confinement. A cage is not a place of confinement but is instead your bird's home. A cage is where the food and water are located, and it provides comfort, protection, and security.

Your bird should come out of the cage everyday. Birds prefer a life with routine and should come out at roughly the same time each day. Extended periods of time outside of the cage will develop expectations on the part of your bird. When these expectations are not met, birds will develop demanding behaviors such as excessive vocalization, throwing food dishes, and hanging on the side of the cage and poop outside of the cage through the bars.

Having the right size cage is critical because pet birds spend a vast majority of their time inside of their cage. They sleep in their cage overnight. They are in their cage during the day when the family is away, and are in their cage at various times throughout the day, such as when the family is cooking or when a dog or cat has access to the bird. For some birds this could mean as many as 15 or more hours per day in their cage. Even if birds can be out all day, such as with retirees or with families who work at home, it does not mean that they should be out all day. Being out all day is not necessarily what your bird needs or wants. Sometimes they want to eat; sometimes they want to rest and sleep; and other times they just want to be left alone. When birds are in their cage they can use all of the different perches, but when birds are out of the cage all day they tend to spend most of their time on a single perch. This situation is uncomfortable and predisposes them to bumblefoot. If birds are sleeping or sitting quietly while outside of their cage, they may prefer the comfort and security of their cage at that time. Inside of their cage, birds have more toys to play with, have more opportunities to forage, and have easier access to food and water. Even if your bird spends a great deal of time out of the cage, your bird needs to return to the cage for opportunities to rest, preen, eat, drink, relax, or contemplate the meaning of life without being disturbed. Admittedly, some birds do okay being out of their cage all day, but even they welcome alone time in their cage. Having birds out of their cage all day does not give them the feeling of being freer, it only makes us feel better to think so, and makes them fell vulnerable.

A common problem with cages is that they are too small. (Figure 4) Small cages are a problem in that they can cause development of unwanted behaviors such as excessive vocalization, throwing food dishes, pooping outside of the cage through the bars, feather damage from rubbing on the cage bars, refusing to come out or go in, and biting.

Figure 4: Housing birds in cages that are too small will lead to health and behavioral problems.

Another common problem is not providing birds with the appropriate style of cage. Housing a bird in an inappropriate style of cage can cause and contribute to behavioral problems such as excessive vocalization, phobic behaviors, biting, aggression, and feather damaging behaviors, among others. Cage styles that should not be used to house birds include play top cages, round cages, and hanging cages. Appropriate cage styles include dome-top, triple-top, and flat-top without the play top and tray. (Figure 5 a, b, c)

Figure 5a, 5b: Triple top and dome top cages are appropriate styles of cages because they provide more interior space than play top cages and discourage birds from playing on top of the cage.

Figure 5c: Flat top cages are an acceptable style, provided there is not a tray or play gym on top.

Play top cages can significantly contribute to these behavioral problems. Play tops are generally too tall for the average owner to comfortably reach their bird when their bird is on top of the cage, making it difficult to get them down. When this happens, a bird will run to the back, climb down the backside, or exhibit some other avoidance behavior to prevent being removed from their place of security. Also play top cages often have trays on top that block light, and they have much less interior space because the dome top has been replaced with a flat top.

Round cages are another style of cage that is to be avoided. (Figure 6a) Round cages should be avoided because they do not give birds a point of reference, which can be disorienting, leading to obsessive behaviors such as continually climbing in circles around the inside of the cage. Round

Figure 6a: Round cages are an inappropriate style of cage that can lead to behavioral and health problems.

cages are always too small; they are difficult to keep clean; they are difficult to set up such that they would have multiple perches that stay clean; they are unsanitary because there is not a grate in the bottom; they are often hung which causes great insecurity for your birds; and the vast majority of commercial pet bird products are not made to attach to the curved surface of a round cage.

Hanging cages are another style to avoid. (Figure 6b) These cages are not safe as they can tip or fall. They do not provide security because the cage swings, which is worse when the cage is being serviced. A cage that is small enough to hang is too small for any bird.

Cage styles with small doors should also be avoided. If the cage has only slide up doors, rest assured that the door and cage are too small. A large door is critical to allow easy removal of your bird from the cage, easy return to the cage, and easy access to the interior of the cage. Birds must be able to come out through the opening on a hand or perch without any obstruction. A door is recognizably too small if birds can grab the header of the door with their beak as they are going in or coming out.

Figure 6b: Birds feel insecure in hanging cages, and they pose a risk of injury to the bird from falling.

Fancy cages such as house-top cages and temple-top cages should be avoided because they are difficult to keep clean; they are too small for the intended size bird; and the doors are too small. (Figure 6c)

Figure 6c: This cage is not only too small, but it is an inappropriate style; the door is too small, and the shape of the top makes it difficult to keep clean.

CHOOSING THE RIGHT CAGE

Qualities of a good cage

a) Powder coated, stainless steel, or aluminum for durability.
b) Large door for easy access to your bird and the interior of the cage.
c) Dome top for maximum interior cage space.
d) Outside access to food dishes.
e) Pull out tray and grate for easy cleaning.
f) Good casters for ease of moving, especially for large cages.
g) Parrot-proof latches to prevent escape.

You need to supply your bird with a safe and comfortable home in which to live. It is vital that you choose a cage that is the appropriate size and bar spacing, and that this home is secure, spacious, and easy to clean. A general rule is to buy the largest cage that you have room for and can afford.

The most obvious consideration when selecting a cage is the size of your bird. At the very least, pet birds need to be able to outstretch and flap their wings to full wingspan when inside the cage. Another consideration is that cages need to be large enough to be furnished properly, complete with food dishes, several perches, several toys, and foraging opportunities. These objects, while absolutely necessary, dramatically cut down the amount of open interior space.

Guidelines for Minimum Cage Size and Maximum Bar Spacing

a) Canaries, finches, and other passerines:
A flight cage is optimal. The cage needs to be wide and not tall.
Minimum size: 24" x 36" with $\frac{1}{2}$" bar spacing

b) Budgies, parrotlets, lovebirds, lineolated parakeets, and similar sized birds:
Minimum size: 20" x 20" with $\frac{1}{2}$" - $\frac{5}{8}$" bar spacing

c) Cockatiels, small conures, and similar sized birds:
   Minimum size: 20" x 24" with $\frac{1}{2}$" - $\frac{5}{8}$" bar spacing

d) Conures, Poicephalus, and similar sized birds:
   Minimum size - 23" x 32" with $\frac{5}{8}$" - $\frac{3}{4}$" bar spacing

e) Small Amazons, Timneh African grey, Pionus, and similar sized birds:
   Minimum size - 24" x 36" with $\frac{3}{4}$" - 1" bar spacing

f) Large Amazons, Congo African grey, and similar sized birds:
   Minimum size - 30" x 40" with $\frac{3}{4}$" -1" bar spacing

g) Small cockatoos, mini macaws, and similar sized birds:
   Minimum size - 32" x 42" with $\frac{3}{4}$" -1" bar spacing

h) Large cockatoos, large macaws, and similar sized birds:
   Minimum size - 36" x 48" with 1" - 1$\frac{5}{8}$" bar spacing

FOR CAGES, DO NOT

Do not house birds in small cages.

Because small cages can lead to behavior problems, such as refusing to come out of and go back into the cage, territorial aggression, hanging from the side and pooping out of the cage, cage destructive behaviors, throwing food dishes, scooping food, excessive screaming, and feather damaging behaviors.

Instead buy the largest cage you have space for and can afford while adhering to minimum cage size recommendations. The larger the cage the better, but be aware of bar spacing and be sure to outfit larger cages with an adequate number of perches. Cages cannot be too large provided they are furnished with enough perches. It is important to note that a large door will provide easy access to reach your bird and to clean the inside of the cage.

Preventive Health Care for Pet Birds

Do not house birds in round cages.
Because birds have no point of reference or orientation without corners and will climb in circles in the cage. Round cages are always too small for the intended size bird. (Figure 7) They are uncomfortable and limit mobility. Round cages are difficult to keep clean because the have no tray or grate (Figure 8) and perches cannot be placed so as to prevent everything underneath from being pooped on. Round cages have small doors making it difficult to get your bird out.

Instead purchase a large rectangular cage with a dome top, large door, and pullout grate.

Figure 7: Round cages are always too small for the intended size bird.

Do not house birds in hanging cages.
Because hanging the cage will make your bird feel insecure. Hanging cages can lead to potential injuries if the cage were to fall. Also hanging cages make cleaning much more difficult.

Instead your cage should be on a secure stand or sturdy table.

Do not cover your cage
Because birds are prey species and if they can hear what could be coming after them but not see it, they become anxious and afraid.

Instead partially cover the cage and leave it covered. Your bird can then retreat into the secure area and still be able to monitor the environment for dangers. If you already cover the cage and have been doing so for some time, then continue to cover it.

Do not house your bird in play top cages
Because allowing birds on top of cages will lead to them having behaviors problems.

Figure 8: Round cages are also difficult to clean because they do not have a tray or a pullout grate.

Instead house your bird in a dome-top cage or rectangular cage without a play top and without a tray on top.

FURNISHING THE CAGE WITH BIRD CARE ESSENTIALS

Perches

Perches are one of the most important furnishings you will put into the cage. There are several different types of perches commercially available. It is recommended to have at least three different types of perches in the cage.

Types of Perches

Natural branches
Use only commercially available natural branches such as Manzanita, Cholla, Sparkle wood, Ribbon wood, Java wood, and Grape wood, among other hardwoods that are commercially available.

Therapeutic Pedicure Perch
This perch will keep your bird's nails short and dull. Pedicure perches also aid in the prevention of bumblefoot, a serious foot disease. Pedicure perches need to be oversize to be effective.

Rope
A spiral rope is the perfect choice for a rope perch. It is a perch and swing all in one and provides hours of fun and exercise for your bird. In addition it allows for more efficient use of cage space, and helps to reduce the amount of cage cleaning needed.

Edible Perches
Edible perches are generally made of calcium carbonate and usually come flavored. These perches are used for beak conditioning and can replace mineral blocks.

Food Dishes

Most cages come with food dishes. In addition to these you need to offer a hanging or mounted dish higher in the cage. This dish needs to be mounted near the highest perch, which provides a more secure and comfortable location for your bird to eat. This higher food dish can be used to convert to a pellet diet and can be used to introduce new foods.

Water bottle

Water bottles are more sanitary than water dishes and provide continuous fresh water to your bird. Water bottles should be washed and refilled daily, and checked at least twice daily to be sure they are working properly.

Toys

Toys are vital to your bird's health and emotional well-being. (Figure 9) A minimum of three toys should be offered in your bird's cage. Hanging one toy per perch is optimal.

Figure 9: Toys are essential to a bird's psychological well-being.

Foraging Feeders and Foraging Toys

Foraging feeders and foraging toys are the most important environmental enrichment that you can provide your bird. Foraging is a natural behavior that provides endless entertainment and is psychologically healthy for your bird.

Substrate

The best substrate to use in a cage is flat paper such as newspaper. Flat paper allows you to monitor your bird's droppings. Changes in droppings can be an early symptom of illness. Put the paper underneath the grate to prevent your bird from having access to the waste products in the bottom of the cage.

FOR FURNISHING THE CAGE, DO NOT

Do not give your bird a tent or hut to sleep in.
Because tents stimulate breeding and nesting behaviors. This will cause an increase in hormones, which can lead to behavior and health problems. (Figure 10)

Instead provide a partial cover over the cage to offer a secure hiding place. If your bird prefers to sleep in a tent, then provide one that hangs over a perch and does not have a bottom. This way your bird can naturally perch and still feel secure.

Figure 10: : Sleeping in tents and huts is a stimulus for reproductive behaviors and disease and should be avoided.

SETTING UP YOUR BIRD'S CAGE

When setting up a cage, start with the perches. The best perches to use are called half perches, which bolt on one end and are free on the other end. (Figure 11) Perches that span the cage make cage cleaning more difficult and divide your cage in half, which often makes bird's not use the lower half of the cage.

Figure 11: Half perches or perches that bolt on only one ends allows for more efficient use of cage space.

The three most important perches are the food dish perch (Figure 12), the water bottle perch (Figure 13), and the sleeping or roosting perch (Figure 14). Perches should be placed to give easy access to the food and water sources. The sleeping perch should be a pedicure perch and placed as the highest perch in the cage so your bird sleeps on it. This perch keeps nails dull and prevents bumblefoot lesions.

Figure 12: Perches allow easy access to food.

Figure 13: Perches allow for easy access to the water bottle.

Figure 14: Start a cage setup by placing a pedicure perch as the highest in the cage.

The remaining perches need to be spaced far enough apart so your bird needs to stretch or hop from one perch to the next. (Figure 15) The perches should be placed in a way that prevents your bird from having to climb on the cage. Obviously your bird will still climb on the cage, but using this as a guideline will ensure that you have enough perches and that they are properly placed.

Bird Care Essentials

The next perch to put in the cage is a spiral rope. (Figure 16) The spiral rope serves multiple purposes. It will provide fun and exercise because it swings and bounces. It also helps to use the cage space more efficiently. With half perches, the center column of cage space is open. This is where the spiral rope hangs and allows easy access to all levels of perches.

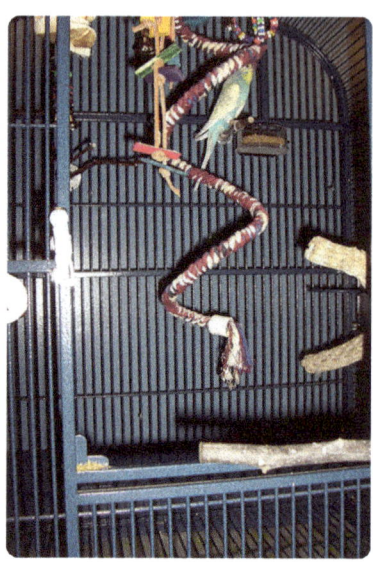

Figure 15: Place perches in empty spots.

Figure 16: Hang a spiral rope to allow easy access to all other perches.

The right cage set up affords your bird comfort and convenience. It is also much easier to clean and maintain a cage that is set up properly. (Figure 17)

Figure 17: The proper cage setup will provide your bird with the optimum amount of cage space and make cleaning much easier.

CAGE LOCATION

Cage location is as important as cage size and style. Cages should not be placed adjacent to an entryway into the room. Persons through the door appear suddenly and startle birds. Individual birdcages should not be kept in a bird room, bedroom, or other similar location that is out of the major traffic areas of the home. These locations lead to feelings of isolation and can cause development of unwanted behaviors such as excessive vocalization, throwing food dishes, phobic behaviors, biting, aggression, chewing cage paint, pooping outside of the cage through the bars, and feather damaging behaviors. Placing cages under stairwells should be avoided to prevent insecurity caused by the thunderous noises generated when using the stairs. Your bird will be much happier to be in the main room of the home where there is lots of traffic and activity. If your bird's cage is placed in front of a window, the cage should be partially covered in front of the window to provide security from the frightening things outside such as hawks, owls, cats, and other scary things.

Cages need to be placed in a very well lit room because birds do not see well in dim light. If a bird is forced to live in low light levels phobic behaviors and insecurity develops, which can lead to biting and other unwanted behaviors.

Also, cages need to be placed with at least one side of the cage against a wall or in a corner. Without the walls for security, birds can feel anxious and insecure. They are prey species and need to see in all of the directions that danger could come from. If all sides of the cage are exposed, then they feel vulnerable.

FOR CAGE LOCATION, DO NOT

Do not keep the cage in a totally dark room at night.
Because your bird needs to be able to see how to get around in the cage if necessary and can see any potential dangers.
　　Instead use a nightlight in the room to provide a small mount of ambient light.

Do not put your bird in a "bird room", back room, basement, or bedroom.
Because cages placed in these locations cause feelings of isolation, which can lead to behavior problems such as screaming and feather damaging behaviors, as well as biting when trying to return your bird to its cage.

Instead place the cage in a high traffic area so your bird can feel like a member of the flock and participate in the activities of the flock.

Do not provide your bird with a separate sleep or night cage.
Because these seem like a nest to birds and will stimulate breeding behaviors and hormone production, leading to behavior and health problems.

Instead leave them in their regular cage at night.

CLEANING AND DISINFECTING THE CAGE

Cleaning and disinfecting your bird's cage are important in a preventive health care program. When done correctly cleaning adds very little time to your daily chores, but contributes tremendously to the overall preventive health care program. Cleaning a cage involves changing the paper in the bottom of the cage and spot cleaning the perches, grate, and toys. Cleaning should be performed daily instead of less frequently. Daily cleaning takes only a few minutes to keep the cage clean. This way, your bird's cage will always be clean. However if the cage is cleaned less often, cleaning is more difficult and the time it takes can be greatly increased.

Cleaning the cage is simply removing the organic debris such as food and poop. Organic debris must be removed before disinfecting because it inactivates most disinfectants. Disinfecting is the act of freeing surfaces from the presence of disease-causing organisms such as bacteria, fungi, yeast, and viruses. Infectious organisms are found abundantly in the environment in which your bird lives. A healthy immune system is he first line of defense against these diseases. A healthy immune system depends on proper nutrition, a good health status, and a clean environment. Even with a healthy immune system, an overload of disease-causing organisms or a constant low-grade exposure to disease-causing organisms can lead to infection and illness. Disinfecting can be done weekly and is an important part of the overall preventive health care program.

FOR CLEANING AND DISINFECTING YOUR CAGE, DO NOT

Do not use household cleaners and disinfectants.
Because practically all household cleaners and disinfectants are toxic to pet birds. They can cause significant respiratory disease, cause damage to eyes from the fumes, and are potentially fatal.
    Instead use commercial bird-safe cleaners and disinfectants that are designed to be used on bird cages.

Do not use vinegar to disinfect the cage and accessories.
Because is not an effective disinfectant.
    Instead use commercial bird-safe cleaners and disinfectants that are designed to be used on bird cages.

Perches: The Importance of Perches

The importance of perches cannot be over emphasized. They are the most important furnishing in a cage. Birds spend nearly all of their time on their feet so they need a wide variety of perches of different sizes, shapes, and textures to provide their feet and legs with exercise, and to prevent pressure sores on feet called bumblefoot or pododermatitis. (Figure 18)

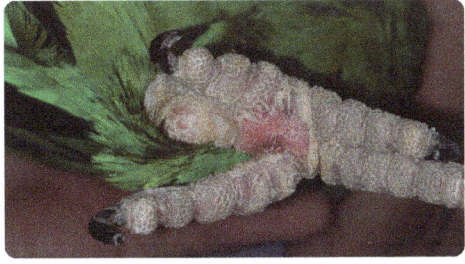

Figure 18: Bumblefoot lesions occur because of a poor diet and inappropriate perches. Smooth perches and perches with a consistent shape should be avoided.

There are several types of perches that are used in bird cages including natural branches, pedicure perches, rope perches, and edible perches. You need to have at least three different types of perches in the cage. The pedicure perch should be the highest perch in the cage so your bird will sleep on it. This prevents bumblefoot and keeps toenails dull.

Bird Care Essentials

FOR PERCHES, DO NOT

Figure 19: Dowel perches are the major cause of bumblefoot lesions.

Do not use wooden or plastic dowels.
Because wooden and plastic dowels are smooth and have a consistent size, shape, and texture. (Figure 19) This type of perch will cause bumblefoot, a painful condition of pressure sores on the soles of the feet.

Instead provide a variety of perches including natural branches, rope, edible, and pedicure perches with varying sizes, shapes, and textures.

Do not use branches from trees outside.
Because branches from outside can expose your bird to deadly parasites, as well as bacterial, viral, and fungal infections. Outdoor branches can also be toxic.

Instead use natural branch perches from reputable bird and pet supplies stores, which have been processed to eliminate dangers. Manzanita, Java wood, dragonwood, and ribbon wood are some of the best choices.

Do not use sandpaper perch covers
Because these are abrasive to feet, cause bumblefoot, and are ineffective at keeping nails groomed. In addition these covers will spin around the perch, which makes the perch insecure. (Figure 20)

Instead use pedicure perches, which are more effective at keeping nails groomed and preventing bumblefoot.

Figure 20: Sandpaper perch covers are abrasive and can cause bumblefoot. They are also insecure because they spin on the perch.

Do not use a sand coated perch for a roosting (sleeping) perch
Because these type of perches are too abrasive for a bird to perch on for long periods of time. Also, these perches are ineffective at grooming nails.

Instead use a pedicure perch made from a lightweight concrete-like material with variability in the surface roughness. The pedicure perch needs to be oversized for your bird's feet and should be the highest perch in the cage.

Water Bottle: The Importance of Water Bottles

WHY TO CONVERT YOUR BIRD TO A WATER BOTTLE.

Bacterial infections are one of the most common health problems that veterinarians encounter in pet birds. The most common source of bacteria is the water dish. An open dish of water is a breeding ground for bacteria. (Figure 21) When left for an extended period dishes will even grow algae. (Figure 22) Organic materials such as food and poop contaminate the water and provide food for the bacteria, which accelerates their growth. Bacterial growth is measured in doubling time, which is the time it takes

Figure 21 and 22: Open dishes of water allow birds to contaminate the water with poop and food. Bacteria grow quickly in this situation and can cause infections in birds.

for bacteria to double in number. Doubling time for many bacteria is only 3-4 hours; so, a clean water dish that is given at 9:00AM will by 1:00PM contain enough bacteria in the water to potentially cause infection and illness. The presence of bacterial contamination is evidenced by the slimy coating on the inside of the dish, called a biofilm, which is a rapidly growing bed of bacteria. Bacterial growth in the water is a health hazard and dirty water is a deterrent to drinking enough to prevent dehydration.

Cleaning a water dish only once or even twice daily is not sufficient to guarantee clean water and prevent major health problems. An awaking rule of thumb is to assess whether or not you would drink the water from the dish. If not, you should not expect your bird to.

Bacterial contamination cannot be managed with water additives such as vinegar. Vinegar is an ineffective disinfectant and may cause birds not to drink the water. A water bottle will effectively prevent water-borne bacterial infections and provide continuous access to clean drinking water.

Most birds will dunk food, bathe, and poop in the water that they are expected to drink. Many owners are concerned that using water bottles will deprive their birds of these activities. Birds are still able to wet their food using the water bottle by dispensing water with food in their beak and without contaminating the water. Birds can be provided with a separate bathing dish that is removed after bathing is over. (Figure 23) A bathing dish can be offered regularly and should be removed within a couple of hours.

Figure 23: A bathing dish can be offered to birds on water bottles. It should be removed after your bird is finished bathing to prevent them from drinking contaminated water.

Birds are dependent on us and we owe it to them to provide the best care available. A water bottle as a bird's source of drinking water is an important part of providing excellent bird care and husbandry, and being proactive in preventing disease. It is a vital part of a preventive health care program. There are no reasons not to put your bird on a bottle.

When using water bottles, a real concern is the possibility that the bottle will malfunction and fail to dispense water. When water bottles are managed properly this problem can be avoided; bottles are safer than drinking dirty water. To avoid these potential problems, it is imperative that water bottles be checked each time they are filled, and at least one other time each day. A good habit to develop is to check the bottle every time you walk by the cage simply by activating the drinker tip ball. The risk of a bottle failing is essentially eliminated by using these husbandry methods.

HOW TO CONVERT YOUR BIRD TO A WATER BOTTLE.

The amount of effort needed to convert to a bottle is small compared to health benefits of drinking from a bottle. When converting your bird to a water bottle, there are some rules that should be used to have a successful conversion. Having the correct size drinker tube size is essential. If the tube is too small, birds will have difficulty getting water and may not convert. Your bird needs easy access to the drinker tube. If the tube is difficult to reach, your bird may not convert. Placement of the bottles is another important factor. The drinker tip should be mounted at your bird's beak-height above a perch and positioned so water does not drip onto the perch. Perches that are constantly wet will develop mold growth.

Converting your bird to a bottle is easy; if hamsters can learn to drink from a bottle, then a bird should be able to. Sometimes simply showing birds where the bottle is in the cage and that it is a water source will be enough to get them to convert. Place your bird on the perch near the drinker tube and tap the ball on the end of the tube to demonstrate dispensing water. Your bird will be curious when water drips, the tube makes a noise, and bubbles emerge in the bottle. When your bird beaks the drinker tip, water will come out, and your bird will realize it is a source of water. You need to repeat this action if your bird does not respond immediately.

If both the bottle and dish are present in the cage, it will be less likely that your bird will convert. Remove the water dish from the cage when the bottle is introduced. Provide water in a dish every three to four hours outside of the cage only. Each time you return your bird to the cage, place your bird on the water bottle perch and demonstrate the water bottle. Continue to offer a water dish only outside of the cage until your bird is consistently drinking from the bottle. You will know that your bird is drinking from the bottle if your bird does not drink from the dish, by observing your bird drinking from it, and seeing evidence of water on the cage bottom.

FOR WATER SOURCES, DO NOT

Do not use water dishes as your bird's drinking water source.
Because water dishes are the most common source of bacterial infections in birds. In an official study at The Birdie Boutique, Inc., water dishes showed significant bacterial growth after only 3-4 hours. Changing dishes only once or twice daily is insufficient for preventing infections.

Instead use water bottles, which are more sanitary. The study at The Birdie Boutique, Inc., demonstrated that water bottles do not show bacterial growth before day 5. However, for the freshest water, bottles need to be changed every 24-48 hours.

Tray Liner: The Importance of Flat Paper Tray Liners

It is best to use flat paper such as newspaper to line the cage tray. Shavings and litter can be a health hazard because of dust, toxins, and growth of infectious organisms. Litter also gives a false sense that the cage is clean since the litter hides the droppings, leading owners to clean the cage less frequently.

FOR TRAY LINERS, DO NOT

Do not use corncob or walnut shell bedding.
Because corncob and walnut shell bedding grow mold and bacteria, especially *Aspergillus* fungus, which can cause infections in birds and

humans. Corn cob bedding also produces an offensive odor when it becomes wet and soiled.

Instead use flat paper such as newspaper. Flat paper does not grow infectious organisms and does not produce an odor. It also allows you to monitor your bird's droppings.

Do not use litters such as pine shavings, cedar chips, or cat litter.
Because droppings cannot be effectively monitored. Litters can be dusty and many contain toxic chemicals. Many times litter will look clean and not get changed for days, which greatly increases the risk of disease in pet birds.

Instead use flat paper such as newspaper. Droppings can be monitored for changes in color, size, consistency, and frequency. Changes in droppings can be an early indication of illness.

Toys: The Importance of Toys

Birds are very intelligent and need stimuli that are fun and occupy their time. Toys are especially important for chewing to maintain a healthy beak, as well as provide exercise to the muscles that operate the beak. Good rules of thumb are to offer a minimum of three toys in the cage or have a toy for each perch. Toys should be rotated regularly to prevent boredom and you should replace the chewed toys. Be sure to offer toys of appropriate size for your particular size bird.

Toys come in many forms. Hanging toys are the most common, but there are toys that mount on the side of the cage or hang from a perch. There are also foot toys that are designed to be held in the foot to play with.

Toys can be made from many different materials such as plastic, wood, metal, rope, palm fronds, yucca, paper, and cardboard. It is important to purchase toys from reputable pet and bird supplies stores to be sure that the toys are made specifically for birds and are safe and non-toxic.

Foraging Feeders: The Importance of Foraging

Foraging is the act of hunting for food. In the wild birds spend up to 70% of their time foraging. In captivity they have open food dishes and spend no time foraging. Foraging is instinctual and birds need foraging activities to be challenged and stimulated. They should work for their food. Foraging is not only mentally stimulating; it also requires a tremendous amount of physical exercise. The ultimate goal is for birds to have no open dishes of food in the cage and forage for all of their food.

Foraging opportunities can be offered with special puzzle-like toys that have to be manipulated to retrieve the food. Foraging can also be accomplished using special food containers that must be opened by a bird to get to the food. For example, there may be drawers to pull out or a cardboard insert that must be torn open to get to the food. Foraging can also be as simple as fruits or vegetables on a skewer. Foraging does not always have to be a food container or puzzle. It can be as easy as multiple dishes placed far apart with only a pellet or a small treat in each one. This way the bird has to go to different areas of the cage multiple times to get enough food, which encourages environmental exploration and promotes the search instinct.

Many commercial foraging toys and feeders are available. However, foraging containers can also be made at home. For example a treat in a paper bag or paper cup that is folded closed works great. A straw with peanut butter inside is a popular forager, too. Hollow a bell pepper and fill it with food and non-food items such as wooden or plastic balls. These non-food items are distracters and increase the amount of foraging time necessary to get the food out.

Lighting: The Importance of Full-Spectrum Lighting

Indoor light is typically provided by electric lighting alone, or in conjunction with natural light passing through glass windows or doors. Incandescent or fluorescent lighting, even when supplemented with natural light, does not provide the quality of bright light necessary for a bird to be happy and healthy because UV rays do not penetrate glass. To improve the quality of indoor light, it is necessary to provide full-spectrum lighting. Lighting should include both bright white visible light and UV light.

UV light is often taken for granted and is often an overlooked environmental necessity for maintaining a happy, healthy bird. UV light is important to birds for three primary reasons. Firstly, UV light improves sight ability for birds. Birds have four different color cones in the eye: red, green, blue, and UV. Without UV light the UV color cones are not being stimulated and birds are considered colorblind. UV light allows birds to see colors that are more natural and recognizable to them. Often birds with UV light will eat foods they have rejected before or accept new toys that had frightened them before.

Secondly, UV light provides birds an important nutritional health benefit. It provides them with a natural source of vitamin D_3. The oil from the preen gland contains a precursor of vitamin D_3. The oil is spread through the feathers when your bird is preening. When the oil on the feathers is exposed to UV light, the precursor is converted to vitamin D_3. As your bird preens, this natural vitamin D_3 is ingested. Consuming natural vitamin D_3 is important to balance the vitamin D_3 in correct ratios with calcium, phosphorous, and trace minerals. Vitamin D_3 deficiency can present with metabolic bone disease (rickets), soft-shelled eggs, egg binding, and neurologic symptoms such as mild to severe tremors, ataxia (wobbling), and even seizures.

Thirdly, UV light improves the quality, strength, and color of the feathers and beak. Healthy feathers are important because they regulate body temperature and protect the body against mechanical damage, actinic sunrays, excessive water, and environmental temperature changes. For all of these reasons, providing UV light will dramatically improve your bird's quality of life and is an important part of a successful preventive health care program.

Not all UV lights are the same. Some emit wavelengths of light that are necessary for humans. There are also different ones for use with plants (horticulture bulbs), with reptiles (herpetological bulbs), and with fish (aquarium bulbs). None of which are suitable for birds. Even if stated on the box, proclaimed by the pet store clerk, or by the manufacturer, none of these are appropriate for birds because they do not provide the wavelengths of UV light that are beneficial to birds. You should provide only UV lights designed specifically for birds.

In order to receive the benefits from natural outdoor UV light, birds need to be exposed to indirect sunlight for 30-45 minutes per day. It is impractical for indoor birds to rely exclusively on natural UV light. They cannot be outdoors enough to benefit from natural UV light exposure. Also, placing them in front of a window does not provide sufficient natural light because the UV rays are filtered out by the glass. Taking them outside for exposure to natural light exposes them to predators, risks of escape, and overheating. Cold weather is also an impractical time to take them out for extended periods of time. With indoor artificial UV light, birds need up to 4 hours of exposure per day. I recommend using a timer set for the light to come on for 2-3 hours in the morning, at or just after sun-up, go off, then come back on for 2-3 hours in the late afternoon or early evening and go off just before sundown. This schedule keeps them on the natural light cycle and does not interrupt their daily eating and sleeping routines.

FOR LIGHTING, DO NOT

Do not keep your bird in dim light.
Because birds cannot see in dim light, which decreases activity and eating, and causes them to become easily startled.
  Instead provide artificial UV light for at least 4 hours per day, preferably split into two 2-hour periods.

Preventive Health Care for Pet Birds

Play Gym: The Importance of a Play Gym

It is vital that your bird come out of his cage regularly. When out, your bird needs a place to hangout and play. Many times a bird can be found on the owners shoulder or on top of the cage. However, it is recommended that your bird does not play on top of the cage and should be on your shoulder for only a limited amount of time if any. These two locations are not recommended because they can lead to behavior problems. A better alternative is to provide your bird with a play gym. Play gyms offer many advantages over cage tops and shoulders. They provide a safe place for your bird to hang out; the play gym can be moved from room to room so your bird can spend more time with you; they are the perfect place to offer snacks; and they are useful when potty training your bird.

Carrier: The Importance of a Carrier

Inevitably you will need to travel with your bird, if to no other place than to the veterinarian. Keeping your bird in a travel carrier is much more safe than traveling with your bird in the open. Without the protection of a carrier, you risk your bird escaping and you expose them to predators.

Gram Scale: The Importance of a Gram Scale

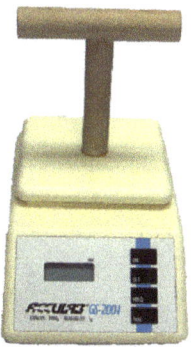

Figure 24: A gram scale is essential for monitoring your bird's health.

Birds are very adept at hiding signs of illness. One of the early symptoms is to stop eating. However, most often they will pretend to eat, making it difficult to know if they are eating or not. Obviously they lose weight when they do not eat. Judging if your bird has lost weight is near impossible without weighing them. You will need a scale that weighs in grams at 1-2 gram increments for an accurate result. (Figure 24) It is

35

a good idea to monitor your bird's weight. You should weigh your bird weekly and keep a log of weights. This way you can establish a baseline weight. If you suspect that your bird is sick, then you should weigh your bird daily. If your bird loses 10% of their body weight or if they lose weight for 3 days in a row, you should have your bird seen by an avian veterinarian as soon as possible. Be sure to take your weight log with you to the veterinarian.

Veterinary Care: The Importance of Veterinary Care

The most important part of a preventive health care program is regular veterinary care. Preventive veterinary care consists of an annual well-bird checkup (includes blood work, physical exam, and fecal Gram's stain), a survey X-ray (radiograph), and having your bird DNA sexed. All of these procedures are used to establish baseline values and to screen for health problems that are hidden or subclinical. Grooming procedures such as nail trims, beak care, and wing feather clipping are also part of complete veterinary care.

It is stressful for a bird to visit a veterinarian but the benefits of seeing a veterinarian outweigh any stress the bird can experience. Stress can sometimes precipitate clinical disease in a bird that is subclinical and make it appear as if your bird became sick after visiting the veterinary office. Keep in mind that it is common for a bird that appears healthy to be diagnosed with subclinical and even clinical disease that the owner is not aware of.

Veterinary Care: The Importance of Veterinary Care

What is an Avian Veterinarian and Why Does My Bird Need One?

The avian veterinarian is one of the most important people in your bird's life, second only to your bird's family. Your avian veterinarian is an excellent source for basic care information, and more importantly, medical care for your bird.

An avian veterinarian is one who sees birds. A veterinarian does not have to see exclusively birds to be an avian veterinarian. With a few exceptions, an avian veterinarian will see other species of pets as well as birds, or can be one who sees mostly birds, and even a few veterinarians will see exclusively birds.

An avian veterinarian acquires the same education as other veterinarians but has an interest in birds and gains knowledge of bird care through continuing education and other extracurricular sources. An avian veterinarian can go further in the education process and become Board Certified. Veterinarians who are Board Certified have proven knowledge and expertise above and beyond what is required to practice veterinary medicine.

Annual Well- Bird Checkups

Health screening is vital to maintaining a healthy bird because birds are very good at hiding symptoms of illness. The annual check up is an important part of a preventive health care program because it establishes a baseline of health parameters for your bird, and because it screens for diseases that your bird could be hiding. The annual check up includes a physical exam, blood work, a fecal Gram's stain, and annual vaccines. Grooming procedures such as nail trim, beak care, and wing feather clipping may also be necessary during the annual visit.

The physical exam is done to realize what your bird looks like when it is healthy and to look for any physical signs of poor health. A thorough exam should include looking in eyes, ears, nares, and oral cavity, listening to heart and lungs, looking at skin condition and feather quality, checking feet for bumblefoot, palpating the abdomen for swelling or distention, checking range of motion of the limbs, and checking the preen gland for enlargement and to be sure it is dispensing preen oil. (Figures 25a-e)

Figure 25a

Figure 25c

Figure 25b

Figure 25d

Figure 25e

Figure 25 a, b, c, d, e: A thorough physical exam is critical to establish a baseline and to screen for health problems. As part of a thorough exam, your avian veterinarian should look at your bird's eyes, ears, oral cavity, listen to heart and lungs, and check feet for bumblefoot.

Annual blood work consists of a complete blood count (CBC), a white cell count (WBC), and a chemistry panel. The CBC provides information on red blood cells including the amount of red cells in the blood, the condition and morphology of the red cells, and the number of thrombocytes, which are involved in clotting blood. The WBC is a primarily a screen for infections. It tells how many total white cells there are in the blood and how many of each type of white blood cell is present. The chemistry panel primarily tests liver and kidney function, the amount of protein in the blood, calcium levels, and amount of glucose in the blood, among other parameters.

Figure 26a: Female Budgie

The cloaca is the location where all of the waste products, which are feces, urine, and urates, collect before being eliminated from the body. A swab sample from the cloaca is representative of the flora of the gut. The cloacal Gram's stain looks for the number and morphology of the gut flora, and screens for subclinical bacterial and yeast infections.

All birds, including individual pets, breeder birds, and adult birds, regardless of exposure to other birds, need to be vaccinated annually against Avian Polyomavirus. The purpose is to remove carrier states from the population, to protect young birds from infection, and to hopefully eradicate this disease-causing virus. Baby birds are particularly vulnerable to infection and should be vaccinated as soon as 30-50 days of age, depending on the species.

Figure 26b: Male budgie

Nearly all parrots are not sexually dimorphic, which means that males and females look exactly the same. In order to determine the sex of pet birds they need to be DNA sexed. DNA sexing is considered a diagnostic tool because males and females have different health issues. There are a few parrots that are sexually dimorphic. Male and female budgies have a different color cere; males are blue, females are brown. (Figure 26a, 26b) The eclectus has the most striking sexual dimorphism; males are green, females are red. (Figure 27a, 27b) There are very few other species that are dimorphic. Knowing the sex of your bird can help your veterinarian rule out gender specific diseases and administer appropriate treatment.

Figure 27a: Female eclectus

Figure 27b: Male eclectus

Grooming may or may not be necessary during your bird's annual checkup. Grooming includes nail trims, beak care, and wing feather clipping. It is uncommon for nails to grow too long, however, sharp nails are common. It is easy to prevent both of these conditions with the right perch. If your bird sleeps on a pedicure perch, they will likely never need a nail trim. Beak trims are uncommon unless the beak is overgrown. Wing feather clipping may or not be necessary for your bird. There are many factors that are involved when deciding if your bird needs to be clipped or not. Each situation is different and it is a personal choice to clip or not. Birds are happier and healthier if they are not clipped. However they are more prone to having behavior problems such

Veterinary Care: The Importance of Veterinary Care

as biting and aggression, and exhibiting independence especially at the wrong times. They are at risk of escaping. They are also at risk of injury such as flying into windows, mirrors, or ceiling fans.

Veterinarians should have survey radiographs (X-rays) of your bird on file to establish a baseline anatomical record. Survey radiographs are also used for screening and early disease detection. Survey radiographs do not need to be repeated annually. It is recommended that a baseline survey radiograph be done before your bird is 3 years of age. If your bird is older than 3 years of age, a survey radiograph should be done as soon as possible, during a time when your bird is considered healthy and free of disease.

How to Know When Your Bird is Sick, and When to See an Avian Veterinarian

Birds are masters at hiding their signs of illness. Pretending to feel well is a survival instinct. When a bird in the flock is sick and the flock is aware, that sick bird will be chased away, ostracized, or physically attacked in order to protect the rest of the flock from predators.

Even though they are in captivity, pet birds retain their natural instincts and hide their signs of illness. Birds can act as if they are normal and feeling well by becoming perky and active when you enter the room or pay attention to them. They may make a slight vocalization, sleek their feathers, may stretch to greet you, and will often pretend to eat. These behaviors make it difficult to determine when your bird is sick. Typically a bird can be sick for 2-3 days before displaying any noticeable signs of illness. If your bird is showing noticeable symptoms, it has become an emergency situation and your bird needs to be seen by an avian veterinarian immediately. Waiting longer to see if your bird improves will only make your bird worse and jeopardize your bird's life. (Figures 28, 29)

Some diseases have specific signs that indicate your bird has a particular disease or injury. However, it is more often the case that your bird will show only general signs of illness regardless of the cause of disease. There is an extensive list of general symptoms. Some symptoms are elusive and occur early in the disease process. Symptoms can quickly become more serious and develop into life-threatening illness.

Figure 28, 29: These are examples of what a sick bird looks like. Generally they are fluffed with their eyes closed and typically standing on both feet.

Typically the earliest indication of illness is that your bird will become quiet. If your bird is typically vocal, like chirping, singing, squawking, or talking, then becomes quiet, especially during those times when you expect your bird to be vocal, then you should make an appointment to be seen as soon as possible. There may also be changes in temperament or demeanor, such as a bird that does not like to be handled, suddenly allows petting and touching; or a bird that is normally affectionate becomes grouchy or even aggressive.

Another early symptom is that your bird will be eating less, or most likely, not eating at all. Be aware that your bird may be pretending to eat. The three best methods to know if your bird is eating are: monitoring weight, monitoring droppings, and observing for visible signs of eating.

The best and most accurate of these methods is by monitoring weight. For this method to be useful, you will need to know your bird's normal weight by weighing regularly and keep a log of the weights for reference. I recommend weighing weekly for a healthy bird. If you suspect that your bird is ill, then daily weights are necessary. If your bird loses weight three

Veterinary Care: The Importance of Veterinary Care

days in a row, or looses 10% of its weight in three days or less, it is an indication that he or she is not eating.

The next method of determining if your bird is eating is to monitor their droppings. You should be monitoring your bird's droppings to become familiar with what is normal for your bird. You should be aware of the normal size of the droppings, the typical color, shape, and consistency, and how many per day there are in the bottom of the cage. Knowing what normal droppings look like helps you to notice when they are abnormal.

Figure 30: Normal droppings

A normal dropping has three different parts: the green portion is the feces, which is from the GI tract; the white portion is the urates, which is from the kidneys; and the liquid portion is the urine, which is also from the kidneys. Normal droppings will be firm and formed, have more feces than urates, and will have just enough urine to make the dropping shiny or cause a small halo of moisture around the dropping. (Figure 30) Droppings can vary depending on many factors, such as what your bird has been eating, whether your bird is molting, your bird's reproductive status, and what time of day the droppings are passed. For example, morning droppings are typically larger, looser, and may even have a slight odor. This variability should only be seen irregularly, with the vast majority being normal droppings. When abnormal droppings occur consistently it indicates that your bird is sick.

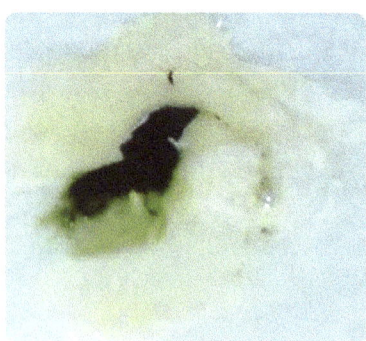

Figure 31: This is the dropping of a bird who is not eating. The fecal portion is dark green, almost black, which is caused by bile in the droppings.

Since sick birds generally do not eat, the feces will turn dark green or even black, or there may not be any feces at all. (Figure 31) Depending on why your bird is sick, there will be other changes to be aware of, for example, there could be no urine or urates or excessive urine; the urates can be yellow or green; the fecal portion can be loose, which is true diarrhea (Figure 32); or the fecal portion can be an abnormal color.

Finally to know if your bird is eating you can look for visible signs that they are eating. You can look to see if there is less food in the dish, see if there are crumbs or empty seed hulls in the dish as well as on the cage bottom, or you can actually observe your bird eating and not pretending to eat.

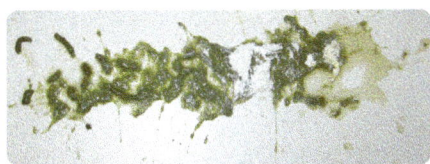

Figure 32: In this picture of diarrhea, the fecal portion is not formed.

Another early symptom to watch for in a sick bird is fluffed feathers and an abnormal posture. Sick birds will fluff their feathers, squat over both feet to cover them with feathers, and have their beak tucked over their back underneath the wing. These positions are to conserve body heat and energy and indicate that your bird no longer has enough energy to stay alert or awake. Birds in this condition are usually on the bottom of the cage instead of on a perch. If your bird shows these symptoms they are in critical condition and an emergency veterinary visit is necessary. Other postures exhibited by a sick bird include drooping tail or wings, leaning forward on the perch, leaning on the cage bars, or hanging by their beak from the side of the cage.

The aforementioned are earlier signs of illness. The following list is a comprehensive list that contains other signs that are typically more apparent and occur later in the disease process. Subtle signs are often missed and should be acted upon as soon as they are noticed. Obvious signs of illness indicate your bird has progressed into a more serious condition and should be treated as an emergency with an immediate visit to your avian veterinarian.

SIGNS OF A SICK BIRD

Not vocalizing
Change in temperament or demeanor
Changes in droppings
Not eating or pretending to eat
Weight loss or prominent keel
Fluffed feathers
Abnormal posture
Sitting on the bottom of the cage
Any visible bleeding
Bare spots or abnormal featherless areas
Being harassed by cage mates
Change in respiratory rate
Change in voice
Changes in feather color
Crusting around or discharge from eyes, mouth, or nares (nostrils)
Difficulty breathing (dyspnea)
Drooping or nonfunctioning limb
Droppings matted to feathers underneath the tail and around the vent
Dull lack-luster feathers
Excessive time spent molting
Head flicking or shaking
Not preening or poorly preened feathers
Open-mouthed breathing
Over-grown or crooked nails or beak
Partially closed, almond-shaped eyes (normally round and open) (Figures 33a, 33b)
Poor or no response to stimuli
Protrusion of tissue or an egg from the vent
Redness or feather loss around eyes
Regurgitating or vomiting
Respiratory noises: coughing, sneezing, wheezing, or gurgling
Sitting in one spot for an extended time
Straining such as to pass an egg or droppings
Swelling of any body part
Tail bobbing when breathing

Preventive Health Care for Pet Birds

Weakness, loss of balance, falling from perch
Wet, stained, or matted head feathers

Figure 33a: Round eyes are normal for a healthy bird.

Figure 33b: Almond-shaped eyes are a sign of a sick bird.

If your bird is sick or injured, before you call your avian veterinarian, move your bird into a small cage or carrier that serves as a hospital cage. Have in the cage an easily accessible perch and easily accessible food and water. Heat up the cage to 90-95°F. A great source of heat is a regular heating pad. Be sure that your heating pad does not have a timed shut off. The heating pad should be placed partially on top and hanging down the side of the cage over the highest perch. Use a towel to cover the cage enough to keep the heat in but do not fully cover the cage to prevent overheating and to allow light bright enough that your bird can easily see to eat and move around in the cage.

FOR VETERINARY CARE, DO NOT

Do not take your bird to the veterinary hospital unless it is in a travel carrier
Because it is not safe and exposes your bird to potential risks. Unless protected inside of a carrier, they are vulnerable to predators, and it provides an opportunity for your bird to escape. Inside of the hospital another bird can injure your bird if it flies over to another cage. A startled bird is likely to fly suddenly, even if the wing feathers are clipped, and be in danger of any of these events no matter how confident you are that your bird will not leave your shoulder.

   Instead travel with your bird in a sturdy carrier.

Veterinary Care: The Importance of Veterinary Care

Do not remove your bird from the carrier at the veterinary hospital until asked to do so by the veterinarian or staff
Because it keeps your bird's stress level lower, prevents injury from other birds or non-avian patients, prevents escape from the exam room and reception area, and makes it easier for the veterinarian or technician to safely restrain your bird.
   Instead leave your bird in the carrier where it is safe and easier to manage.

Do not fill your bird's carrier with toys and perches.
Because it makes catching your bird in the carrier very difficult and risks injury to your bird.
   Instead put only one perch in the cage and no toys.

Do not put water in your bird's cage when visiting the veterinary office.
Because the water spills and will prevent correct assessment of the droppings in the bottom of the cage. Your bird should not have water before the exam to prevent aspiration while being handled.
   Instead provide water after the droppings have been assessed and your bird has been examined

Do not feed your bird before your visit.
Because it is more difficult to take a blood sample when a bird has a full crop. A full crop increases the risk of aspiration during handling. Your bird may need to be anesthetized for X-rays or other procedures. A full crop increases the chance of your bird becoming car sick.
   Instead remove your bird's food from the cage the night before your visit if you have morning appointment, or the morning of your visit if it is an afternoon appointment. Smaller birds like budgies, cockatiels, and small conures should be fasted for 4 hours; larger birds should be fasted for 8 hours.

Do not change the paper in the bottom of the cage before your visit
Because your veterinarian needs to see your birds droppings to help determine why your bird is sick.
   Instead do not clean the cage, or save the droppings from the previous 24 hours if you do clean the cage

Do not use over-the-counter (OTC) medications, home remedies, or other medications not prescribed by your avian veterinarian.
Because the medications are ineffective at treating disease. They can give you a false sense that your bird is improving only to find that your bird relapses and becomes worse. OTC medications may not be safe for your bird. OTC antibiotics can lead to resistant bacteria.

Instead Use only the medications prescribed by your avian veterinarian.

Do not put multiple birds in one carrier
Because it is difficult to remove one bird from the carrier without the other bird escaping.

Instead have only one bird per carrier.

Avian First Aid: Be Your Bird's First Responder

Avian first aid is defined as the initial treatment given to a sick or injured bird while awaiting veterinary medical care. It is administered in emergency medical situations to stabilize the patient until complete veterinary medical care can be provided. First Aid is not a substitute for qualified avian veterinary care. A medical emergency is a serious, potentially life-threatening injury or illness that requires immediate attention. If you are unsure of the severity of your bird's condition, it should be treated as an emergency.

Avian First Aid: Be Your Bird's First Responder

Emergency situations requiring immediate veterinary attention

a) Bleeding that cannot be stopped
b) Blood in droppings or in regurgitant
c) Burns
d) Unable to breathe
e) Unable to keep balanced or falling from perches
f) Ingested a foreign body
g) Poisoning
h) Puncture wound or deep cut
i) Sitting on the bottom of the cage
j) Straining to pass droppings or an egg
k) Attacked by a cat, dog, or other predator

Emergency situations requiring same-day veterinary attention

a) Diarrhea
b) Excessive sleeping
c) Excessive thirst
d) Excessive urination
e) Eye injury or irritation
f) Fluffed
g) Loss of appetite
h) Noticeably sick bird
i) Self-mutilation
j) Showing lameness in legs or wings
k) Sudden swellings any place on the body

Preventive Health Care for Pet Birds

How to Manage Emergency Situations

Emergencies invariably happen so you need to be prepared. If you are prepared you will better be able to manage the situation when an emergency does occur. Being prepared means that you have everything you need ready to manage the emergency. The two most important items to have ready are a first aid kit and a hospital cage.

THE FIRST AID KIT

Commercial kits are available or you can put one together yourself. Here is a list if supplies you need for your first aid kit.
- a) Betadine to clean wounds
- b) Bottle of eyewash to rinse eyes and wounds that have been contaminated.
- c) Cotton balls
- d) Cotton-tipped applicators or swabs
- e) Gauze
- f) Hydrogen peroxide to clean blood off of feathers and skin (not to be used on wounds)
- g) Latex gloves to protect from spreading harmful bacteria found on your hands.
- h) Metal nail file for filing nails and beak that may be sharp, too long, or damaged.
- i) Rubbing alcohol to help keep feathers clear of the working area and as a cooling agent in hyperthermic patients
- j) Scissors for cutting bandage material and feathers
- k) Tweezers to remove wound debris and to clean blocked nares.

HOSPITAL CAGE

A Home Hospital Cage is one of the most important items you will need in case of an emergency or sick bird. It needs to be set up and ready to use at all times, complete with a perch, water bottle, food dishes, and paper in the tray. You will also need a heating pad and some towels. The Hospital Cage can also serve as the carrier to transport your bird when going to the avian veterinarian.

There are a number of different types cages and incubators that will work as a hospital cage. The important points are that the cage can be kept at a constant temperature of 90-95°F and allows easy access to food and water. A small cage will work (Figure 34) as will a plastic aquarium (Figure 35) and even a glass aquarium with a top.

Figure 34: A small cage works great as a hospital cage.

When using an aquarium, the heating pad should be placed underneath one end and up the side to heat one end of the container. A towel should cover the container on the heated end to hold in the heat. When using a small cage, the heating pad needs to be placed on top of the cage over the perch and draped down the side of the cage near the perch; then cover the heating pad with a towel to hold in the heat. The heating pad should be set on high and remain on for 24/7 during the treatment period.

Figure 35: A small plastic aquarium works great as a hospital cage.

WHAT TO DO IN AN EMERGENCY

Basic steps for handling any emergency:
1) Remain calm
2) Remove your bird from the danger
3) Retrieve your first aid kit and supplies
4) Restrain your bird
5) Assess your bird's condition
    a) If your bird is bleeding, then stop the bleeding

      b) If your bird is not breathing then place your bird on a towel in the hospital cage and go immediately to an avian veterinarian.

      c) If your bird is not conscience then place your bird on a towel in the hospital cage and go immediately to an avian veterinarian

4) Administer First Aid and General Supportive Care.
5) Call your veterinarian for further instructions.

GENERAL SUPPORTIVE CARE

General supportive care is administered in all cases of sick and injured birds. It is used to stabilize your bird until veterinary care can be given. General supportive care includes putting your bird into a hospital cage with heat to 90-95°F, providing easy access to food, water and a perch, providing enough light to stimulate eating and drinking, and observing your bird for changes in its condition. Keep your bird quiet and calm and do not handle your bird.

Emergencies Requiring First Aid

a) Animal attacks
b) Bleeding
c) Breathing difficulties
d) Burns
e) Egg Binding
f) Eye problems
g) Fractures
h) Head trauma
i) Heatstroke
j) Sick Bird
k) Toxic inhalation

ANIMAL ATTACKS

Injury by other animals is common with pet birds and can be very serious. There are several species that are found to attack birds including other pet birds, dogs, cats, ferrets, hawks, and raccoons. The best prevention for animal attacks is to prevent exposure to these other animals. Wild animal and outdoor animal attacks can be prevented by always using a carrier when taking your bird outside for any reason and never leave your bird outside unsupervised for any period of time. Other pet birds generally attack out of aggression, mate aggression, territoriality, and jealousy. Most commonly the injuries are to the beak and feet. In worst cases the upper beak is severed and toes are amputated. One of the most dangerous animals that get to birds are cats. Cats carry a bacteria on their teeth and claws that can be fatal to birds. Death from infection can occur in as little as 24 hours. If your bird has been exposed to a cat, you need to rush to the veterinarian for immediate treatment. Even if you are not sure or think your bird was not harmed, go anyway.

First aid steps for animal attacks:
1) Stop the bleeding, if any is present.
2) No other aid can be recommended.
3) There are no other home treatments that are effective against serious infection and internal injuries.
4) Go immediately to the veterinary hospital.

BLEEDING

Bleeding is generally the result of trauma or injury. Blood can originate from beak, nails, feathers, or skin. Any blood loss is always a concern.

However, healthy birds have remarkable clotting abilities and they can tolerate large losses of blood.

General first aid steps for bleeding:
1) Determine the source of the bleeding.

2) If bleeding is minimal, put pressure on the wound until the bleeding stops, then put your bird in a hospital cage and observe to see if the bleeding has stopped.
3) If bleeding stops, make an appointment to have your bird seen as soon as possible for any further necessary medical treatment.
4) If bleeding does not stop within 5 min, administer specific First Aid (See below).
5) After bleeding has stopped, leave your bird in the hospital cage to restrict activity and observe your bird for 1 hour to be sure bleeding does not start again.
6) If you cannot stop the bleeding, if it starts back within 1 hour, or if your bird is weak and listless, call your veterinarian immediately.

Figure 36: A blood feather is an immature feather that contains blood vessels and nerves in the shaft. It is distinguished by the dark color of the shaft. A mature feather has a clear or white shaft.

A Blood feather is an immature feather that is actively growing. It is noticeable by having a dark shaft. The darkness is caused by the presence of blood in the shaft. (Figure 36) Trauma to a blood feather can cause it to break and bleed. (Figure 37)

First aid steps specific for bleeding broken blood feathers:

Do not pull a broken blood feather
1) If the broken feather is no longer bleeding, put your bird in the hospital cage and observe for 1 hour to see if it starts again.
2) If it does not start again, take your bird in for the next available appointment for assessment and any necessary treatment.

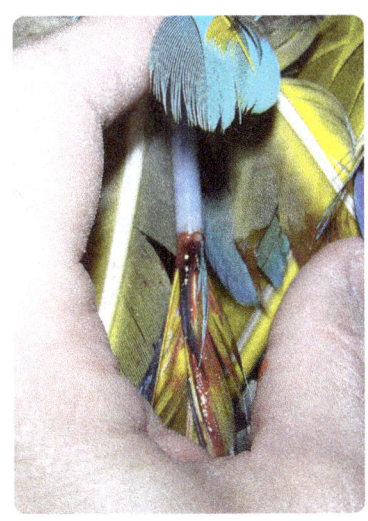

Figure 37: A broken blood feather needs to be treated as an emergency, and bleeding should be stopped as soon as possible. Do not pull a blood feather.

3) If the feather is bleeding, wipe away the blood, apply styptic and direct pressure for 2 minutes or until bleeding stops.
4) Leave your bird in the hospital cage to restrict activity, provide General Supportive Care, and continue to monitor for 1 hour.
5) If this does not stop the bleeding, or bleeding starts back within 1 hour, then take your bird into the veterinarian's office immediately.

First aid steps specific for bleeding from minor skin wounds:
1) Wipe the blood so you can see where the bleeding is.
2) Remove any dirt, feathers, or foreign debris with tweezers and flush with warm saline or eyewash.
3) Apply direct pressure with gauze or paper towel for 2 minutes or until bleeding stops.
4) Clean the wound with Betadine and flush with warm saline to rinse.
5) Apply topical antibacterial spray or cream.
6) Leave your bird in the hospital cage to restrict activity and provide General Supportive Care
7) Call your veterinarian for the soonest available appointment.

BREATHING DIFFICULTIES

Dyspnea or difficulty breathing is potentially life-threatening situation. All cases of dyspnea need to be seen immediately.

Signs to watch for:
a) Coughing
b) Cyanosis or turning blue
c) Nasal discharge
d) Open-mouthed breathing
e) Respiratory noises
f) Tail bob
g) Voice change

First aid steps for dyspnea

1) Provide General Supportive Care.
2) Minimize stress and avoid handling.
3) Contact your veterinarian to be seen immediately.

BURNS

Burns can be very serious and very painful. They can be caused by:
   a) High heat - hot liquid or grease, steam, open flame, or hot surface
   b) Acids - tile cleaners, swimming pool additives, and battery fluid
   c) Alkaline – lye, ammonia, oven cleaners
   d) Chemicals - bleach, phosphates in household cleaners
   e) Electricity - chewing electrical cords

First aid steps for burns
1) Provide General Supportive Care
2) For hot liquid, steam, open flame, or hot surface burns spray or immerse the affected area in cool water to relieve the pain. Allow the area to dry, then apply an antibiotic cream.
3) For hot grease burns apply a light coating of flour or cornstarch before rinsing with cool water. Allow the area to dry, then apply an antibiotic cream.
4) For acid burns apply a light coating of baking soda paste, which is baking soda mixed one to one with water. After cleaning the area allow the area to dry, then apply an antibiotic cream.
5) For alkali burns apply a light coating of vinegar. Rinse with water, then allow the area to dry, then apply an antibiotic cream.
6) For Chemical burns – rinse the area with water, allow the area to dry, then apply an antibiotic cream.
7) For electrical burns - Apply an antibiotic cream.
8) In all burn cases see an avian veterinarian immediately or as soon as possible.

EGG BINDING

Birds generally lay eggs without difficulty. However, occasionally an egg will become stuck and cannot be passed. Stuck eggs can cause kidney, respiratory, and intestinal problems and can rapidly become life threatening.

Signs to watch for
- a) Abdominal swelling
- b) Blood, egg, or red tissue visible from the vent
- c) May be on the cage bottom, backed into the corner with her tail in the air
- d) Panting, difficulty breathing
- e) Paralysis, stiffness, or weakness in legs
- f) Straining
- g) Weak, depressed, or fluffed, appears exhausted

First aid steps for egg binding:
1) Provide General Supportive Care.
2) Increase the humidity by using steam in a bathroom or a warm air humidifier.
3) Take your bird to see an avian veterinarian immediately.

EYE PROBLEMS

Although eye problems are generally not life threatening, all eye problems should be considered potentially serious. Even a minor injury or irritation, if not treated in a timely manner, can progress rapidly, potentially leading to blindness. Ocular lesions are most commonly the result of injury or infection.

Signs to watch for:
- a) Swollen lids.
- b) Lids closed for long periods of time.
- c) Lids pasted closed.
- d) Excessive tearing or ocular discharge.
- e) Increased or excessive blinking or squinting.

f) Rubbing eye, beak, or side of face.
g) Cloudiness of the eye.

First aid steps for eye problems
1) Restrain your bird and carefully examine the eye using light and magnification.
2) If the lids are pasted together, or if there is a discharge, have your bird seen immediately.
3) If there is no discharge, gently open the eye and look for a foreign body; flush with saline eyewash.
4) Contact your veterinarian to be seen as soon as possible.

FRACTURES

Fractured bones are always caused by trauma. Common causes include birds being stepped on, mishandled, attacked by another animal, being closed in a door, and many other forms of trauma. The most common fractures are to the tibiotarsus or shin bone, and the radius and ulna of the wing. At-home repair should not be attempted. Bandages alone are not effective and can do more harm than good, especially if they are applied incorrectly.

Signs to look for:
a) Non-weight bearing, holding up leg
b) Difficulty perching or climbing
c) Drooped wing
d) Swelling and bruising at the fracture site
e) Floppy or functionless limb

First aid steps for fractures
1) Provide General Supportive Care.
2) Put in a hospital cage; remove the perches and line the bottom with a towel.
3) Do not handle your bird unnecessarily, further injury could result.
4) Call your veterinarian immediately.

HEAD TRAUMA

Head trauma usually occurs from flying into a wall, mirror, window, or ceiling fan. Even if there are no signs of injury immediately after the accident, signs can appear later, even becoming fatal.

Signs to watch for:
- a) Depression
- b) Loss of balance
- c) Weakness in legs or wings
- d) Unusual or involuntary movements
- e) Convulsions or seizures
- f) Loss of consciousness
- g) Sleeping more than usual

First aid steps for head trauma
1) Place in a hospital cage, remove the perches, and pad bottom with a large towel.
2) Do not provide heat.
3) Cover most of the cage, dim the lights, and avoid making loud noises.
4) Call your veterinarian immediately.

HEATSTROKE (HYPERTHERMIA)

Over heating occurs when the ambient temperature is too high. For example if birds are left outside in the summer, especially in the direct sun. Overheated birds go into shock very quickly. Heatstroke can cause neurological deficits, seizures, permanent brain damage, and death.

Healthy birds should not be left in temperatures above 90ºF for extended periods.

Signs to watch for
- a) Panting, open-mouthed breathing
- b) Holding wings out from the body
- c) Sleeked feathers

d) Weakness
   e) Convulsions or seizures
   f) Loss of consciousness

First aid steps for heat stroke
   1) Remove your bird from the hot environment.
   2) Place your bird in a cool area.
   3) Spray with cool water and wet feathers to the skin.
   4) Swab rubbing alcohol on your bird's feet.
   5) Offer cool oral electrolyte solution, even putting a few drops inside the beak if your bird is conscious.
   6) Call your veterinarian immediately.

SICK BIRD SYNDROME

Although not often thought of as an emergency, sick birds are one of the most common emergencies. When birds are showing signs of illness, it indicates that they have been sick for at least 2-3 days. At this point a bird is critical and emergency treatment is necessary. Regardless of the disease, all sick birds show the same set of symptoms. This set of non-specific symptoms is referred to as the Sick Bird Syndrome.

Signs to watch for:
   a) Fluffed
   b) Loss of appetite
   c) Listless, inactive, or sleeping more than normal
   d) Change in appearance and/or number of droppings
   e) Not vocalizing
   f) Weight loss

See also *Signs of a Sick Bird* on page 46

First aid steps for a sick bird
   1) Provide General Supportive Care
   2) Providing heat (90-95°F) is the most critical treatment
   3) Call your avian veterinarian to get an appointment as soon as possible

TOXIN INHALATION

Birds have very sensitive respiratory systems and they are more sensitive to inhaled toxins than other animals and people. In addition to respiratory system damage, eyes can be irritated with the chance of developing a corneal ulcer.

Sources for toxic inhalants
  a) Aerosols
  b) Bleach and ammonia
  c) Glues and adhesives
  d) Household cleaners
  e) Kerosene and gasoline
  f) Nail polish remover
  g) Paint and spray paint
  h) Paint thinners and removers
  i) Plug-in air fresheners
  j) Polytetrafluoroethylene and other non-stick coatings
  k) Tobacco smoke

Signs to watch for:
  a) Constant blinking
  b) Coughing
  c) Cyanosis or turning blue
  d) Eyes closed
  e) Open-mouthed breathing
  f) Respiratory noises
  g) Sneezing
  h) Tail bob
  i) Voice change

First Aid for Toxin Inhalation
  1) Get your bird into fresh air immediately.
  2) Call your veterinarian immediately.

TOXIN INGESTION

There are many environmental toxins that your bird is exposed to. Without supervision it is possible that your bird could ingest one of these toxic substances.

Sources for ingested toxins:
    a) Jewelry
    b) Metal
    c) Paint chips
    d) Plastic
    e) Tobacco products
    f) Some plants
    g) Household products such a cleaners, and detergents

Toxic foods
    a) Avocado
    b) Chocolate
    c) Fruit pits and fruit seeds
    d) Alcohol
    e) Coffee
    f) Caffeine

Signs to watch for:
    a) Depressed, Listless, lethargic, or inactive
    b) Feather damaging behaviors and self-mutilation
    c) Regurgitating and vomiting
    d) Tremors and seizures

First aid steps for toxin ingestion:
    1) Remove the source
    2) Call pet poison control hotline 888-426-4435
    3) Contact your avian veterinarian

FOR FIRST AID, DO NOT

Do not pull a broken blood feather
Because it is very painful and traumatic for your bird. It can damage follicles and may cause abnormal replacement feathers. Pulling a blood feather does not stop the bleeding and will often times make bleeding worse. The bleeding starts deep within the follicle where it cannot be reached and forms a hematoma. These can be painful and have the potential for becoming infected. A new blood feather will soon replace the pulled feather and have the potential for also being broken. The broken blood feather will mature quicker than a new feather, so the risk of breaking again is much lower.
 Instead leave the broken blood feather in place and apply a styptic and direct pressure.

Do not use styptic on open wounds
Because it is painful. Applying styptic to an open wound could cause infection. Styptic is not meant for open wounds.
 Instead, apply pressure to stop the bleeding, clean the wound, and apply an antibiotic cream.

Do not use heat for a head trauma
Because heat will cause increased blood flow to the brain, which will exacerbate the swelling caused by the head trauma.
 Instead place your bird in a hospital cage without heat and see your veterinarian immediately.

Do not use mineral oil for an egg bound bird
Because mineral oil does not help since it does not reach the egg when applied to the vent. At home, the oil cannot be placed far enough into the cloaca to be beneficial. Mineral oil will be spread on the feathers with preening and make them unable to keep your bird warm.
 Instead provide your bird with warm humidity and then see an avian veterinarian.

Do not use a heat lamp for warmth.

Because sick birds need a continuous source of heat and lights can not be left on 24 hours per day as your bird will not get any rest. Heat lamps are a focal heat source and do not warm the environment. Heat lamps can cause dehydration, dry skin, dry eyes, and potentially cause burns on bare areas such as the face, beak, and feet.

Instead use a heating pad. Heating pads will disperse the heat more evenly and not cause burns, dry eyes, or dry skin. Be sure to use a heating pad that does not have an automatic shut off.

Do not use your body heat to warm your bird

Because birds have a body temperature of approximately 105°F. Since human body temperature is well below that, instead of heating your bird, it actually will chill your bird. In addition, sick birds should not be held as this is very stressful and they will not get enough rest.

Instead place your bird in a hospital cage where the temperature can be maintained at 90-95°F.

Do not use over-the-counter (OTC) medications, human medications, or medications prescribed for other pets.

Because these medications are not meant for birds and it is very easy to give the wrong dose. In particular, OTC antibiotics should not used because of the potential for creating drug resistant bacteria.

Instead Provide general supportive care and see avian veterinarian who can diagnose your bird's ailment and prescribe the best treatment.

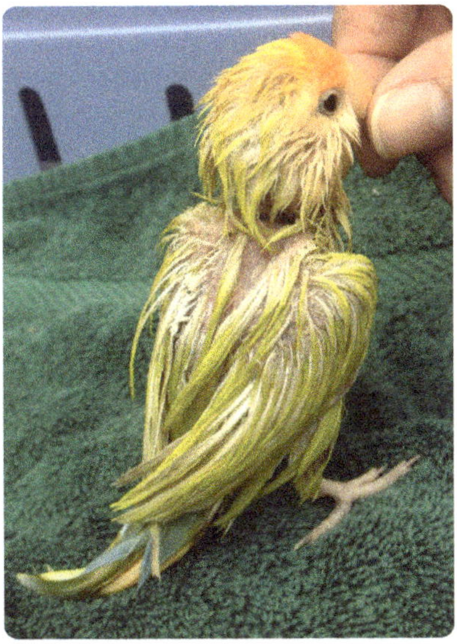

Figure 38 : Ointments should never be used on birds. Oily substances will mat feathers.

Do not use greasy ointments.

Because ointments will contaminate the feathers and reduce your bird's ability to stay warm. (Figure 38)

Instead use only water-soluble creams or sprays. Apply them only with a cotton swab or gloved finger.

Do not bathe a sick bird.
Because it will make your bird cold and stressed. Two things a sick bird does not need.

    Instead wait until your bird is well before giving a bath.

Environmental Toxins

Environmental Toxins

Heavy Metals

ZINC

Zinc poisoning in pet birds has become a very common problem. Heavy metal poisonings in general are an ongoing problem in veterinary medicine, with lead and zinc poisoning being the most common causes. Although lead poisonings are seen in pet birds, parrots tend to be exposed to zinc more than lead because of the perch and toy hardware that is currently used in bird cages.

Zinc toxicosis is primarily an environmental issue and several environmental sources have been identified. Recently, manufacturers have become more aware of the problems with the zinc issue and are now offering safe alternatives, such as stainless steel, and hard plastic hardware. Cages are also being extensively tested for zinc and other heavy metals.

Sources of Zinc
    a) Cage paint, esp. white
    b) Galvanized wire
    c) Hardware cloth
    d) Perch hardware
    e) Rubber
    f) Toy hardware

Signs to watch for
    a) Ataxia
    b) Convulsions
    c) Depression
    d) Diarrhea
    e) Hematuria (blood in urine)
    f) Polydipsia (excessive thirst)
    g) Polyuria (excessive urination)
    h) Seizures
    i) Tremors

j) Weakness
k) Weight loss

The diagnosis of zinc toxicosis is determined by using physical exam results, X-rays, blood testing, and detailed historical information about your bird's environment. Physical exam findings include neurologic deficits, anemia, dermatitis, poor feather quality, loss of appetite, weight loss, and diarrhea. X-rays are taken to determine if there are metal foreign bodies in the GI tract, and a blood sample is submitted to test for the levels of zinc in the blood, which is an important part of the diagnostic work up.

Successful treatment of zinc poisoning is dependent upon early detection. Treatment options are limited to oral medications, called chelators, which remove the toxins from the blood and eventually from the bone and liver. Improvement in a bird's condition can be noted on day 2 or 3 of treatment. For long-term cure of zinc toxicosis any foreign bodies must be removed from the GI tract to prevent chronic toxicosis.

The first life-saving step when preventing zinc toxicosis is to remove the source of zinc from a bird's environment. Test all toy and perch hardware. Replace the hardware that tests positive with stainless steel, acrylic, or other hard plastic hardware options. To test objects for zinc you will need muriatic acid, 2 disposable plastic containers, gloves, and mask. Testing for zinc is an easy straightforward procedure.

Steps for testing objects for zinc
1) Begin by putting on the gloves and mask.
2) Place the article being tested into a small disposable plastic container to prevent spillage onto other surfaces.
3) Apply a few drops of muriatic acid to the object to be tested.
4) Then move the tested item into a container with water to stop the reaction of the muriatic acid with the zinc.

If there are bubbles and foaming then the test is positive for zinc, the object is toxic to your bird and should be removed from your bird's environment. If you find objects that are positive for zinc, then it is strongly recommended to have your bird tested for zinc.

LEAD

Lead is another heavy metal that is commonly found in the environment and is very toxic to pet birds. Although lead is generally not found in bird cages or bird products, there are many environmental sources of lead.

The diagnosis of lead toxicosis is determined by using physical exam results, X-rays, blood testing, and detailed historical information about your bird's environment. Physical exam findings include neurologic deficits, anemia, dermatitis and poor feather quality, loss of appetite, weight loss, blood in the droppings, and diarrhea. X-rays are taken to determine if there are metal foreign bodies in the GI tract. A blood sample is submitted to test for the levels of lead in the blood.

All sources of lead should be removed from your bird's environment. Sources can be determined using an over-the-counter lead test kit found in most hardware stores.

Sources of Lead
- a) Artificial turf
- b) Batteries
- c) Bells with lead clappers
- d) Bird toys weighted with lead
- e) Candy, imported from Mexico
- f) Canned food, imported
- g) Carpentry nails
- h) Ceramics, glazed
- i) Costume and toy jewelry
- j) Curtain weights
- k) Folk medicine
- l) Fumes from leaded gas
- m) Ink, some colors
- n) Lead paints
- o) Lead shot and bullets
- p) Lead sinkers
- q) Leaded crystal
- r) Linoleum

s) Mini blinds
t) Mirror backing
u) Pewter
v) Putty and caulking compounds
w) Radiators
x) Sindoor
y) Soil
z) Solder
aa) Stained glass windows
ab) Tiffany lamps
ac) Toys, imported
ad) Water (contaminated)
ae) Wine bottle foil tops
af) Wrought iron welds on some wrought iron

Signs to watch for:
a) Ataxia
b) Convulsions
c) Depression
d) Diarrhea
e) Hematuria (blood in urine)
f) Polydipsia (excessive thirst)
g) Polyuria (excessive urination)
h) Seizures
i) Tremors
j) Weakness
k) Weight loss

Toxic Foods

Parrots are omnivorous, meaning they eat a wide variety of foods including fruits, vegetables, meat protein, and grains. There are however a few foods that are toxic to them and should never be offered. These include:
a) Alcohol
b) Apple seeds

c) Avocado
d) Caffeine
e) Chocolate
f) Dairy products
g) Fruit pits
h) Garlic
i) Onions
j) Salt
k) Xylitol

Tobacco

Tobacco is especially toxic when ingested. Tobacco is laden with nicotine and countless other chemicals that are toxic to pet birds. The smoke from burning tobacco is also toxic because of the chemicals in the tobacco. Even if you smoke outside or away from your bird, when you handle your bird, the nicotine and other toxins on your hands and cloths are absorbed through your bird's skin on their feet, as well as transferred to the feathers where it can be ingested when your bird preens. Exposure to smoke and chemicals from smoking tobacco can cause respiratory disease, allergic reactions, dirty feathers, and dermatitis. If nicotine levels are high enough it can even cause death.

Teflon and other Non-stick Surfaces

Do not use Teflon® and other non-stick cookware in your home because they emit deadly fumes that is undetectable by humans, but can kill birds nearly instantly.

COMMON ITEMS HAVING TOXIC NON-STICK COATINGS

a) Bread makers
b) Broiler pans
c) Burners on stovetops
d) Cake pans
e) Clothes irons
f) Coffee makers
g) Cookie sheets
h) Corkscrews
i) Crock pots
j) Curling irons
k) Deep fryers
l) Drip pans for burners
m) Electric skillets
n) Griddles
o) Hair straighteners
p) Hairdryers
q) Heat lamps
r) Hot air popcorn poppers
s) Ironing board covers
t) Lollipop molds
u) Many cooking utensils
v) Microwave popcorn bags
w) Muffin tins
x) Non-stick rolling pins
y) Paint
z) Pizza pans
aa) Portable heaters
ab) Roasters
ac) Scotchgard® waterproofing and stain resistant spray
ad) Self-cleaning ovens
ae) Stockpots
af) Tortilla presses
ag) Waffle irons
ah) Woks

Plants

Houseplants are terrific to have. They help clean the air and they produce oxygen. However, many of them are toxic to pet birds. The safest thing to do is avoid keeping toxic plant species. But, if you keep these plants do not allow your bird to have access to them because birds will be tempted to chew on plants without realizing that the plant is toxic.

TOXIC PLANTS

Avocado
Azalea
Black locust
Blue-green algae
Castor bean
Christmas cherry
Coffee beans, tea, chocolate beans
Daffodils
Elephant's ear
English ivy
Ergot
Foxglove
Jerusalem cherry
Jimsonweed
Lilies
Lily of the valley
Locoweed
Milkweed
Mistletoe
Nightshade
Oak
Oleander
Parsley
Philodendron
Poinsettia

Pokeweed
Potatoes
Rhododendron
Tobacco
Tulips
Virginia creeper
Yew

SAFE PLANTS

African violet
American Bittersweet
Aloe
Areca palm
Autumn Olive
Australian laurel
Bamboo
Bamboo palm
Barberry
Bayberry
Beech (American, European)
Begonias
Bird's nest fern
Bladdernut
Blueberry
Boston fern
Bottlebrush fern
Canary Island palm
Christmas cactus
Coffee tree
Comfrey
Coralberry
Corn plant
Cotoneaster firethorn
Crabapple
Creeping fig

Danish ivy
Devil's ivy
Dogwood
Dragon tree
Elderberry
European fan palm
Fiddle leaf fig Fig tree
Fir (Balsam, European, Red)
Flame nettle
Grapevine
Hawaiian schefflera
Huckleberry
Indian laurel
Jade plant
Kangaroo vine
Lace fern
Lady palm
Maidenhair fern
Marigold
Ming fern
Mother fern
Mother-in-law's tongue
Nasturtium
Norfolk pine
Paradise palm
Parlor palm
Pepperomia
Pine (Ponderosa, Spruce, Virginia, White)
Prayer plant
Purple passion
Pyracantha
Raspberry
Rose
Rubber tree
Spider plant
Spruce (Black, Norway, Red, White)
Umbrella tree

Viburnum
Wandering Jew
Wax Plant
White Poplar
Willow

Mite Protectors and Sprays

Mite protectors and mite sprays are still commonly sold in pet stores despite the fact that they are a health hazard for pet birds. Not only are they a health hazard; they can cause dermatitis, respiratory disease, and cancer. In addition these products are ineffective for treating and preventing mites and other parasites. Mite treatment and prevention products are typically unnecessary because pet birds almost never have mites and budgies are the only species of parrots that I have diagnosed mites on. Instead of using over the counter treatments, you should have your bird seen by an avian veterinarian for a correct diagnosis for the symptoms you are seeing and for correct treatment for any condition your bird may have.

Proper Handling and Training

Living with a companion parrot is fun and exciting, but it can also be challenging. How you handle your bird will determine both the amount of fun you and your bird have and how challenging it will be to manage your bird's behaviors. Proper handling and training are part of an overall preventive health care program and are the best ways to prevent behavior problems.

Proper Handling and Training

Wing Clipping

Whether or not to clip your bird's wing feathers is a personal choice that should be made with your bird's safety in mind. Flighted birds are at risk of crashing into windows, mirrors and ceiling fans and at risk of escaping. Flighted birds are healthier and happier. But, flighted birds develop behavior problems such as aggression and independence, making handling and managing your bird more difficult. Having your bird clipped will eliminate the risks associate with being able to fly such as escaping and risk of injury.

It is important to know which feathers to clip. Knowledge of anatomy will be sure you clip the correct feathers. The correct feathers to clip are the primary flight feathers or the remiges. There is never a need to clip secondary feathers or tail feathers or rectrices. (Figures 39a, 39b)

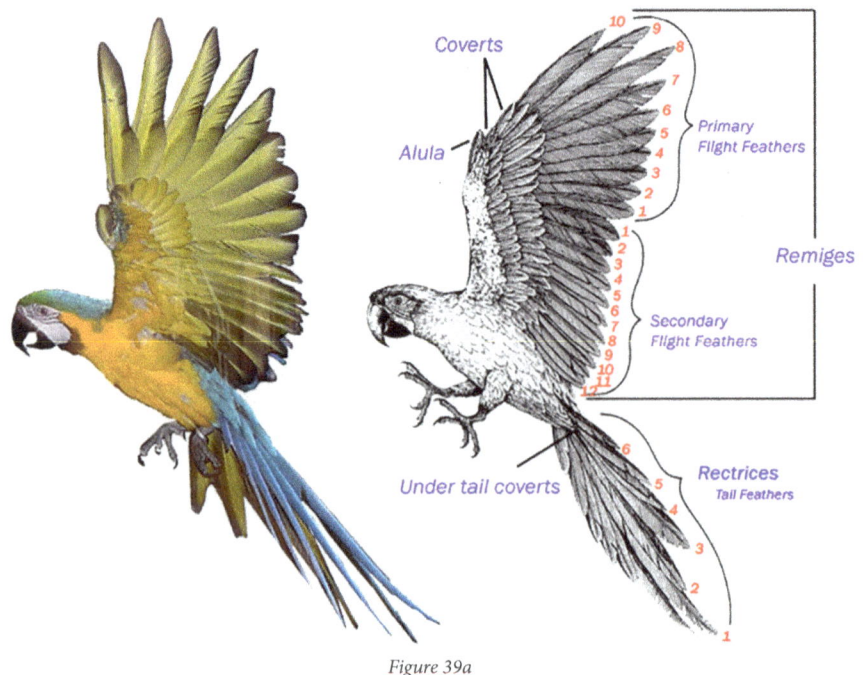

Figure 39a

Preventive Health Care for Pet Birds

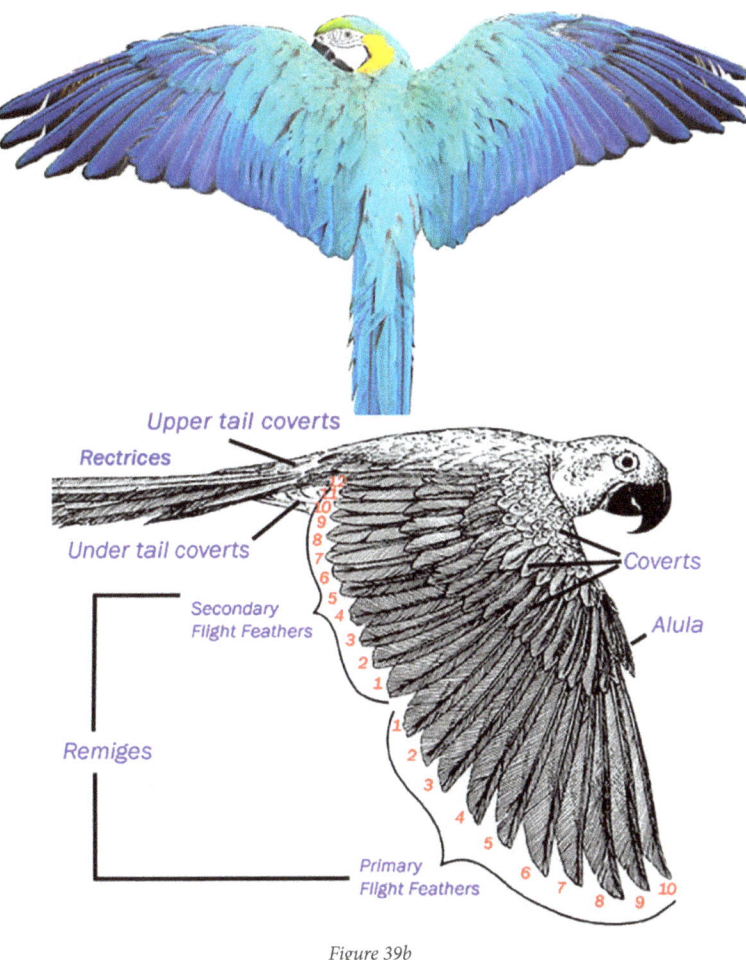

Figure 39b

Figures 39a, 39b: The primary flight feathers are the correct feathers to clip for a safe wing clip.

There are a number of types of wing clips, however, there is only one correct way with variations depending on the kind of bird being clipped. The correct way is to clip 4-6 primaries on each side shorter than the coverts, cutting one feather at a time to prevent sharp edges. (Figure 40a, 40b) The number of primaries that should be clipped depends on the species of bird and their flight ability. A heavier bird, like an Amazon parrot may only need 3 or 4 taken off on each side. A lightweight strong flyer like a cockatiel will require more feathers to be clipped, on average 5-6 on each side.

Figure 40a: Before primary flight feathers are clipped

Figure 40b: After primary flight feathers are clipped

There are many styles of wing clips that are incorrect because they can lead to injury from falling to the floor when trying to fly or losing their balance and falling. (Figures 41a, 41b, 41c)

Figure 41a: Too many wing feathers have been clipped and the clipped feathers are left too long, with sharp edges. This type of wing clip will result in the bird falling to the floor, and it is uncomfortable to the bird. This type of clip has been known to be one cause of feather-damaging behaviors, such as plucking and over preening.

Figure 41b: This clip is referred to as the "cosmetic clip" or "A" clip. This bird is still able to fly because the outer primary flight feathers are intact.

Preventive Health Care for Pet Birds

FOR WING FEATHER CLIPPING, DO NOT

Do not clip your own bird's wings
Because handling your bird the way is necessary for a safe wing clip will cause your bird to lose trust in you and affect your relationship negatively.

Instead have your bird clipped by your avian veterinarian.

Do not clip more than 4-6 primaries on each side
Because clipping too many with prevent a soft glide to the floor without crashing and causing injury.

Instead clip only what is necessary to prevent flight, but leave enough to prevent falling and crashing to the floor.

Figure 41c: The unilateral clip is the most dangerous of all of incorrect clipping. With only one side clipped, the bird is going to spiral to the floor with great risk of injury.

Handling

If your bird is going to coexist with you in a mutually peaceful and loving relationship, your bird needs to be taught some basic commands and some manners. Basic commands include 'up' to your hand, 'down' to a perch, 'stay' where you put your bird, and 'come', using whatever keywords you want to use. These commands allow you to be in charge and manage difficult situations.

Manners include no biting, no aggressive behaviors, no pooping on you or your furniture, and doing what is asked of your bird. Biting and aggression are unacceptable behaviors for the obvious reasons; it is painful and it hurts your feelings. These behaviors also take the joy out of having a companion parrot. Manners are learned over time and behavior problems are generally prevented with proper handling. The most often handling mistakes that can lead to such behaviors are allowing birds on shoulders and on cage tops.

Trick Training

Parrots are highly intelligent and very active. Left to their own accord this energy and intelligence are a recipe for getting into trouble. This energy needs to be channeled into productive behaviors. Trick training is an excellent way to dissipate energy and challenge your bird. It also prevents boredom and provides quality time to spend with your companion. The tricks you can teach your bird are practically limitless. There are some commercial props that are fun such as basketball hoops and puzzles. There are also some parrot agility props available that offer the additional advantage of making your bird exercise. You can also devise tricks at home with homemade props like stacking cups, playing the shell game, or just teach simple tricks like spin on a perch, recall, talking on command, and fetching.

Potty Training

Although bird poop has no odor, and is relatively harmless, few people are willing to venture into public with it on their shoulder for friends to notice and say "Hey, I'll bet you have a pet bird". True bird lovers understand that occasionally their loving pet will poop on them and they accept it with grace and dignity. Nonetheless, I believe that all pet birds should be well mannered, and pooping on people is not good manners. Therefore, I feel that potty training should be employed for a happier coexistence with your pet bird.

It is true that you can potty train your bird. Don't expect your bird to return to their cage when they has to eliminate, but they will be able hold it for reasonable amount of time until you can get them to a place that they are allowed to poop.

The principle behind this training technique is that your bird needs to relieve itself every 15 to 20 minutes. The technique is simple. Each time you take your bird out of their cage, immediately place your bird onto its playpen or training perch. As you are waiting for your bird to poop, repeat a key word that you will use to trigger the event. One of our customers says "Do your poopie". Another uses "Go poo poo". Any word you choose will work. The key words are important because they will be a cue to let your bird know what you expect. If your bird does not go within 2 to 3 minutes, take your bird off of the perch for a couple of minutes. Then place your bird back onto the perch until they go. Repeat the process until your bird poops. Your bird is not allowed off of the perch for any extended period of time until they have pooped. Your bird's reward is getting off of the perch to be with you. Lots of verbal and physical praise is important when they go where they are supposed to go. You can also use a food reward. While your bird is out of their cage, it is important to return them to the training perch every 15 to 20 minutes, make them stay there, and repeat the key word until your bird poops. When your bird poops, their reward is coming off of the perch to be with you and to receive more praise and petting, or get a food reward. Once your bird begins to recognize the key word, you can say it before you remove your bird from the cage and they will learn to poop before they come out.

Utilizing this technique, being patient, being persistent, and keeping on schedule will potty train your bird in 2 to 3 weeks. Potty trained does not mean that your bird will return to the cage or playpen to poop, although some birds will. Potty-trained means that your bird will hold its poops for a reasonable period of time (30 to 45 minutes depending on the size of your bird) until they are put in a proper place to relieve themselves (on a playpen, training perch, or in their cage). Potty-trained also means that your bird should poop on command by using a key word as mentioned earlier. This is very handy when you take your bird to friends' or families' homes. You should be able to hold your bird over a sink, trashcan, or other appropriate receptacle and tell your bird to poop, thereby leaving the friends, family, and carpet free of unwanted poop stains. This technique works!

FOR BEHAVIOR AND HANDLING, DO NOT

Do not allow birds to ride on shoulders or play on top of the cage
Because shoulder rides and cage top play can lead to behavior problems such as avoidance behaviors and biting when trying to remove them from your shoulder or the cage top.

Instead keep them on your hand or lap; they can stay on a play gym and still provide company and companionship. This way you can pet and physically interact with your bird more easily.

Do not allow birds to come and go in and out of their cage on their own.
Because this allows them to make the decision of whether or not to come out or go back in. Birds are not capable of making such decisions. If they decide they do not want to come out, then forcing them out can cause fear, avoidance behaviors, biting, and aggression. Allowing your bird to come and go can make them feel as if they are in charge, which leads to difficult handling and other behavior problems such as being cage bound and cage territorial. Although very intelligent, parrots should not be allowed to make their own decisions because they may not always make the right one.

Instead of letting them come out on their own, reach into the cage to bring them out perched on your hand. When returning your bird to the cage, place them on a perch inside the cage. Having a door perch makes getting them out and putting them in much easier.

Do not travel in a vehicle unless your bird is in a carrier.
Because accidents are more likely to be injurious or fatal, and your bird has the potential to be a distraction. Your bird could be startled and flail, fly inside of the car, or fall into the floor under the pedals.

Instead have your bird in a carrier that is buckled in to insure safety.

Do not take your bird outside unless in a carrier.
Because predators such as hawks and feral cats are a threat. Escape is also a threat. If something frightening happens such as a loud noise, your bird's instinct is to fly. No matter how much you feel that your bird loves you, a bird will not return for love. Even if clipped, they can fly enough to be in danger.

Instead keep your bird in a carrier or travel cage when going outside.

Index

Index

A

Alcohol 65, 73
Amazons 16
Animal attacks 55
annual check up 38
appetite 52, 63, 71, 72
Avian First Aid 51
Avian Polyomavirus 40
Avian Veterinarian 38, 42
avocado 11
Avocado 65, 74, 76

B

bacteria 24, 27, 30, 40, 49, 53, 56, 67
beak 14, 18, 28, 29, 31, 33, 37, 38, 41, 45, 46, 53, 56, 61, 63, 67
Beak trims 41
Behavior 88
behavior problems 16, 24, 35, 41, 81, 85, 88
behaviors 11, 12, 13, 16, 20, 23, 24, 42, 65, 81, 85, 86, 88
Bird Care Essentials 3, 5, 6, 18
bird room 23, 24
Bleeding 52, 55, 56
blood feather 66
blood work 3, 38, 40
Board Certified 38
Breathing difficulties 55
Breathing Difficulties 58
broken blood feather 66
Budgies 15
bumblefoot 12, 21, 25, 26, 39
Burns 52, 55, 59

C

Caffeine 65, 74
cage 5, 6, 8, 9, 10, 11, 12, 13, 14, 15, 16, 17, 18, 19, 20, 21, 22, 23, 24, 25, 27, 29, 30, 31, 32, 35, 44, 45, 46, 47, 48, 52, 53, 55, 57, 58, 60, 61, 62, 66, 85, 86, 87, 88
Cage 13, 14, 15, 20, 23, 24, 25, 53, 70
Cage Location 23
Canaries 15
cat litter 31
cedar chips 31
Chocolate 65, 74
Cleaning 24
cloaca 40, 66
Cockatiels 16
cockatoos 16
Coffee 65, 75, 76, 77
Congo African grey 16
conures 16, 48
corncob 30
Coughing 58, 64
Cyanosis 58, 64

D

dairy 11
Diarrhea 52, 70, 73
Diet 6
diseases 7, 24, 38, 41, 42
disinfecting 24
DNA sexed 37, 41
DNA sexing 41
dowels 26
dropping 44
droppings 10, 20, 30, 31, 43, 44, 46, 48, 52, 63, 72
Dyspnea 58

E

eating 6, 8, 9, 10, 11, 34, 35, 43, 44, 45, 46, 55
Edible Perches 18
egg 33, 46, 52, 60, 66
Egg Binding 55, 60
egg bound 66
Emergencies 53, 55

emergency 42, 45, 51, 53, 54, 63
Escape 88
eye 33, 60, 61
Eye problems 55
Eye Problems 60

F

finches 7, 9, 15
First Aid 51, 53, 55, 57, 64, 66
follicle 66
Food Dishes 19
Foraging 5, 19, 32
Foraging Feeders 19
Foraging Toys 19
formulated pellet 6, 7
Fractures 55, 61
Full Spectrum Lighting 33

G

General Supportive Care 55, 58, 59, 60, 61, 63
Gram Scale 35
Gram's stain 38, 40
grit 10
Grooming 37, 38, 41

H

Handling 85, 88
hanging cages 13, 17
Hanging cages 14, 17
Head trauma 55, 62
heat lamp 67
Heatstroke 55, 62
heavy metal 72
hospital cage 47, 55, 67
Hospital Cage 53, 54
Husbandry 3

L

Lead 72
lovebirds 15

M

macaws 16
Mite Protectors 79
molting 44, 46
monitoring weight 43

N

nail trims 37, 41
Nasal discharge 58
Natural branches 18
newspaper 20, 30, 31
Non-stick 74, 75

O

Open-mouthed breathing 46, 58
OTC medications 49
over-the-counter 49, 67, 72

P

parrotlets 15
pedicure perch 21, 25, 27, 41
Perches 18, 20, 21, 25, 26, 29
physical exam 3, 38, 71, 72
pine shavings 31
Plants 76
Play Gym 35
Play top cages 13
Poicephalus 16
Potty Training 86
predators 34, 35, 42, 47, 88
preventive health care program 3, 5, 6, 24, 28, 34, 37, 38, 81

Index

R

Rope 18
round cages 13, 17
Round cages 13, 17

S

Safe Plants 77
sandpaper perch covers 26
Scale 35
sex 41
shoulders 35, 85, 88
sick bird 42, 45, 52, 63, 68
Sick Bird 55, 63
Signs of a Sick Bird 46
signs of illness 35, 42, 43, 45, 63
Sources of Lead 72
Sources of Zinc 70
style of cage 13
styptic 58, 66
Substrate 20
Supplements 6

T

Tail bob 58, 64
Teflon 74
territorial 16, 88
Therapeutic Pedicure Perch 18
Timneh African grey 16
Tobacco 64, 74, 77
Toxic foods 65
Toxic Foods 73
Toxic inhalation 55
Toxic Plants 76
Toxin Ingestion 65
Toxin Inhalation 64
toxins 64, 65, 71, 74
Toys 19, 31, 73
Tray Liners 30
treat 6
Trick Training 86

U

UV light 33, 34

V

vaccinated 40
veterinarian 3, 10, 35, 36, 37, 38, 41, 42, 45, 47, 48, 49, 54, 55, 56, 57, 58, 59, 60, 61, 62, 63, 64, 65, 66, 67, 79
Veterinary Care 37, 47
vinegar 25, 28, 59
vitamin D 33
vitamins 11
vocalizing 46, 63

W

walnut shell bedding 30
water 11, 12, 19, 21, 27, 28, 29, 30, 34, 47, 48, 53, 55, 59, 63, 67, 71
Water bottle 5, 19
Water Bottle 27, 29
water dish 27, 29
Weight loss 46, 63, 71, 73
well-bird checkup 37
windows 33, 42, 73
Wing Clipping 82
wing feather clipping 37, 41
Wing feather clipping 41

X

X-rays 3, 42, 48, 71, 72

Z

Zinc 70
zinc poisoning 70, 71
zinc toxicosis 71

www.ingramcontent.com/pod-product-compliance
Lightning Source LLC
Chambersburg PA
CBHW042118100526
44587CB00025B/4107